More ADVENTURES OF THE HORSE DOCTOR'S HUSBAND

More ADVENTURES OF THE HORSE DOCTOR'S HUSBAND

JUSTIN B. LONG

Published in the United States by Springhill Media
Newberry, Florida, USA
https://SpringhillEquine.com

SPRINGHILL

Cover & Book Design: mycustombookcover.com
Limits of Liability and Disclaimer Warranty:
The author shall not be liable for your misuse of this material. This book is strictly for entertainment purposes.

First edition printing February 2020

ISBN 978-1-948169-26-4 (Ebook Edition)
ISBN 978-1-948169-27-1 (Paperback Edition)
ISBN 978-1-948169-28-8 (Hardcover Edition)

Library of Congress Control Number: 2019920776

For Erica, who lives fearlessly
and loves unconditionally

Other books by Justin B. Long
Adventures of the Horse Doctor's Husband
How to Become an Equine Veterinarian: A Guide for Teens
(co-authored by Dr. Erica Lacher)

THE DIMWORLD SERIES
Genesis Dimension
When Good Plans Go Bad
Inside The Machine

Contents

Chapter 1

Introductions Are in Order

IF YOU HAVEN'T READ THE FIRST BOOK in this series, *Adventures of the Horse Doctor's Husband*, then I'll take a minute and get you caught up on all the important stuff, like who I am, and what this is all about. You'll probably want to read that book too, but if this one is in your hand and that one isn't nearby, we'll go with what we've got. You gotta start somewhere, right?

My name is Justin Long, and I'm married to Dr. Erica Lacher, a famous equine veterinarian in the horse world. A lot of people around the world listen to our podcast, *Straight from the Horse Doctor's Mouth*, which is all about horse health, and how to make the world a better place for your horse. We own Springhill Equine Veterinary Clinic in Newberry, Florida, which Erica has been captaining since 2006. I married into all this; she did the hard work.

The first book has the long version of how we met, our amazing costume wedding (she was Lara Croft, Tomb Raider, and rappelled out of a tree to the altar rather than walking down the aisle. I was King Arthur from Monty Python), and how I ended up in this job, so I'll make this version short and sweet.

Like many people do, I picked the wrong person on the first try. Or, maybe she was the right person for me at that point in my life and helped me get to the next phase of my life, I don't know. She was (and still is) a wonderful person, but we stopped being right for each other at some point. So, after twelve years, at the ripe old age of 33, I found myself single, almost two years sober, and on an intense path of self-discovery and personal growth. I give a ton of credit to my mentor and my therapist for helping me evolve into a much better version of me than I had been up to that point. I worked my ass off too, and I've learned that it's important to acknowledge that. I was a group project.

When I was 38, I felt like I might be ready to try to find my soulmate. I had a few false starts, which is reasonable, since I hadn't dated in 18 years. My best friend, Kristen, convinced me to try out eHarmony.com and see who else was out there in the world. There was no one that matched me in my town, or even in the whole state of Georgia. A last-ditch nationwide search in June of 2014 showed two really strong matches. One lived in Oregon, and one lived in Florida. I started with the one in Florida, since that was reasonably close. Her name was Erica, and while I was excited to find her, I had absolutely no way of knowing how much she was going to change and improve my life. (Spoiler alert: It was a LOT!)

My therapist had helped me develop a list of things I was looking for in a partner, and as I got to know Erica, I determined that she met all thirty-one of my criteria. She was incredible in every way. At this point in my life, my struggling self-confidence wasn't sure what she saw in me that she liked so much, but my therapist helped me avoid sinking my own ship with all the nonsense that goes on in my head. We dated for nine months before I moved to Florida, and when we'd been together for a year and a half, we got married.

My job plan in the beginning was to work somewhere else and stay removed from the veterinary clinic. That was Erica's thing, and I didn't know much about it. I certainly didn't want to barge in there as Erica's new husband and start screwing things up.

I don't know if it was coincidence or divine intervention, but I didn't find a job somewhere else. I have a pretty diverse skill set, but I just wasn't finding what I was looking for. Erica finally convinced me to start helping at the clinic. She needed someone to handle the bookkeeping and pay bills, run errands, and so on, and with some training, I stuck my toes in the water. It turns out that the water was fine, just fine.

I'm still the bookkeeper and errand runner, and now I manage the financial side of the business. I produce our podcast, which comes out on the 1st and 15th of every month. I built our website, along with a few others, which I manage as a side business. Most importantly, at least for me, I get to write books. I have a science fiction series called *The DimWorld Series* that I'm very excited about. I'm working on the fourth book in that series now. I also get to go out with Erica and have all these adventures, which I then get to write about and share with you. It's a great fit for me in every way, and something that

I never could have built for myself. Like I said, Erica changed and improved my life in ways I never could have imagined. For that, I will be forever grateful.

Something important that I want to talk about briefly is the collection of stories you're about to read. We are an active veterinary clinic, and the people and animals I'm about to tell you about are real. For their privacy, I have changed names, locations, and any other personal details that might divulge their identity. There's a fine balance between sharing the struggles that horse owners go through and airing out people's personal business, and I work very hard to maintain the trust that people have built with our team. I even changed the names of our staff. Some of these stories feature one of our other veterinarians, and I have changed their names, too. My goal is that if you and your horse are in this book, no one will know it but you and those you choose to share that insight with.

The other important note is about my explanations of the medicine that's being practiced. I am not a veterinarian, and this is not a step-by-step description of how things are done. While I try to explain what's going on in each situation, there are undoubtedly many important steps that I fail to mention. Sometimes it's on purpose, as it just bogs down the story. Other times it's because I forgot something that happened, since it was a 2:00 am emergency from three years ago. You understand what I mean, right?

This is an adventure story, not a medical textbook. If some of the practices I describe are different from the way your veterinarian does it, don't run out and beat your vet up about it! There are often a variety of ways to do things. Also, medical practices change over time as new technologies and understandings become available. Your vet might be behind the times. Then again, we might be behind the times. There's nothing wrong with asking questions about things, and as an involved horse owner, you should be asking questions. I just don't want you to attack someone over something I've said, that's all. No one responds well to that.

Just to recap, here are the important things you need to know going into this story:

- Dr. Erica Lacher is a real-life Wonder Woman.

- Dr. Erica Lacher is tough, strong, compassionate, caring, intelligent, and amazing.

- Justin Long has the best job in the world, and he knows it.

- You should check out their podcast, *Straight from the Horse Doctor's Mouth.*

- This is not a medical textbook. This is an adventure story about horses (and a few other critters), their owners, and their veterinarian.

- By the end of this book, you may want to move to Florida so that Erica can be your vet. This is a normal response. Do not be alarmed.

I think that covers it. You might want to explore our website at some point. We have a great weekly blog called *Tuesdays with Tony*, written by our clinic cat, Tony. Our YouTube channel has a lot of good videos, and it's linked on our website, too. This is all free, by the way. It's part of our mission, which is to make the world a better place for horses. Find it all at SpringhillEquine.com and follow us on Facebook!

Okay, here we go. Enjoy!

Justin B. Long, November 2019

Chapter 2

IF YOU MESS WITH THE BULL, YOU GET THE HORN

EVERY ONCE IN A WHILE, I haul a client horse into the clinic for treatment. Usually it's a colic, and not very exciting, other than the fact that colicky horses don't tend to poop in the trailer. As the official trailer cleaner, I notice little things like that. This wasn't going to be one of those horses.

We use a group chat app on our phones called GroupMe at the veterinary clinic. It's a great way for us to communicate with each other throughout the day when everyone is scattered to the four winds. It's also a great way for me to stay plugged into the action, as I work from home a lot. It's messages like this that really catch my eye:

Horse gored by bull in Jonesville. Dr. Russel, you are closest, can you go after your current appt?

We see an emergency of some sort almost every day, but this was a first for me. I was at my desk, paying bills and watching the sheep eating my mother-in-law's flowers across the driveway when the message came in. I totally wanted to race over there and see the horse, just to be nosy, but it wouldn't be very professional, so I kept working, hoping that they would post pictures so I could see.

About thirty minutes later, my phone buzzed again, with a special chime that lets me know that someone tagged me in a GroupMe message.

Justin, are you available to haul a horse to the clinic?

It was Dr. Russel asking. I was going to see the horse after all!

Just so there's no confusion about my excitement, let me explain. I hate to see any animal in pain or suffering from an illness or injury. That's not the kind of person I am at all. When it does happen, though, there is something very interesting and satisfying about seeing the extent of an injury, and then witnessing the miracle of modern medicine as the doctors bring the horse back to health. All animals are incredible in their own way, but horses seem to be exceptional in their ability to produce spectacular injuries and amazing recoveries, and that's something I never get tired of witnessing.

I typed a quick reply as I jammed my feet into my shoes and raced downstairs.

On my way. Shoot me an address.

I hadn't been down this road before, so I took a quick peek at the place on Google Maps before setting out. An ounce of prevention is worth a ton of cure when pulling a big horse trailer into an unknown area, and I know better than to drive blindly into a place without knowing how I'm going to get back out. Trailering 101.

The farm was behind a subdivision, near the end of the road. The image was a few years old, but it didn't look like the kind of place that would have changed much. There was a big field in front of the house, and I could tell from the tire tracks all over it that it wasn't fenced. You can't ask for more than that.

It took me about ten minutes to get there. When I turned onto the street, I knew at once that Google Maps hadn't been able to see one important detail. The canopy of trees overhead hid the fact that the road was one of those fancy gated subdivision roads, a divided two-lane that weaves back and forth for no apparent reason. Whoever designed the road clearly didn't own a trailer or consider that someone else might have to pull one through here. The corridor was straight as an arrow, so the road was built this way purely for appearances.

With the truck tires hanging off the right side of the pavement and the trailer tires hanging off the left, I began creeping down the road, craning my neck to make sure the trailer didn't scrape the trees that lined the narrow winding lane. I didn't have to go far, maybe half a mile, so that was good. I couldn't go more than ten miles per hour, so it seemed like it was further than that. Finally, the entrance to the subdivision appeared, with its giant ornamental black gates. Once I passed that, the road turned into a normal street, straight and wide. I shook my head.

Another quarter of a mile, and I found the farm. Dr. Russel's vet truck was nowhere in sight, so I stopped out in front of the house and looked around. It was an old rambling farmhouse, two-story with a wrap-around porch. It had clearly been here a lot longer than the subdivision, and I guessed that the subdivision had once been part of the farm. There were a variety of outbuildings and sheds, and a maze of fences between them. Dr. Russel's truck had to be back there somewhere, but how it got there was a mystery to me. I picked up my phone to call her when it beeped in my hand.

Hang on, I'm coming to get you.

The message was from Cassie, Dr. Russel's technician. A moment later, the vet truck popped around a corner and zigzagged through the pens. I climbed out of my truck and slid into the passenger seat of the vet truck.

"Hi!"

"Hey. I don't think you can get the trailer back there, but let me show you where she is."

I knew by the first corner we turned that there was no way the trailer was going through there. I doubted that I could even get the truck back there. With four doors and an eight-foot bed, it turned like a school bus, and never mind the thirty-foot trailer. A minute later we emerged in a field. To the left, there were some cows standing around a water trough. Several of them were bulls, and all of them had horns. Only one of the bulls was genuinely big. The others were much smaller, although when talking about bulls, that's a relative statement. They swished their tails and watched us with lazy eyes as we drove by.

To the right, at the far end of the pasture, Dr. Russel was standing with a horse and two people. Cassie swung the wheel and made her way to them, dodging rocks along the way.

"Is it bad?" I was suddenly worried that the horse might not be able to walk out to where the trailer was. If that was the case, we were going to have a serious problem. "Can she walk?"

"Well, the wound is pretty deep, but she's walking on it okay. Dr. R. is trying to see if it hit anything vital before we move her, though."

We parked close by and hopped out. An older couple stood to the side, watching as Dr. Russel probed the wound in the horse's shoulder.

"Whew, it looks like somebody's having a bad day," I said with a grin. "I'm Justin Long. Sorry to meet you like this."

"Thank you so much for coming. I'm Sadie, and that's my husband, Reggie." Sadie stepped forward and shook my hand. She was strikingly beautiful. Her skin was the color of milk chocolate, and her jet-black hair was pulled back in a tight bun. She gestured to the horse. "This here is Cinnamon. She tried to steal the bull's breakfast this morning."

"That sounds like a bad plan." I watched in awe as Dr. Russel slid her hand inside the horse's shoulder, all the way to her wrist.

"She's never done that before," Reggie grunted. "Been living together for five years, never had a problem."

Cinnamon's breathing began to slow as the pain meds kicked in. I couldn't imagine how much pain she was in, but it had to be a lot.

"He warned her twice," Sadie said. "I was watering the plants on the back porch when she walked over there and stuck her nose in his food. He snorted at her, and she stepped back, but then she did it again, and the third time is when he got her. It wasn't even a hard hit. He didn't get a run at her or anything, they were both standing still. He just kinda headbutted her."

"It probably doesn't take much momentum when you weight fifteen hundred pounds." I shook my head. "That's a tough start to the day."

Sadie blew out a breath, half laugh and half sigh. "Tell me about it. We're supposed to be flying out in a few hours for a conference this weekend."

Dr. Russel finished her examination just then and stepped back, pulling off her gloves. "I don't know how they managed it, but somehow there's nothing serious here other than the damage to the muscles. If it had gone any deeper, we'd be looking at internal bleeding and possible organ damage, so she got lucky."

"So, she's going to make it?" Reggie reached up and scratched Cinnamon between the ears. The stress falling from his face was visible, and I realized that he'd been pretty sure she wasn't going to survive.

"Oh yeah, she's going to be fine," Dr. Russel said with a grin. "I'm going to cover the wound to keep it clean on the trailer ride, and once we get her to the clinic, I'll stitch her up and get her in a stall. When you get home from your conference, we'll bring her back. It'll take some time to heal, but she'll be fine."

Reggie wrapped his arms around Sadie, and they stood there for a moment, silent. I helped Cassie get all the bloody gauze cleaned up while Dr. Russel covered the wound. A few minutes later, we began the slow walk up front.

Cinnamon walked pretty well, considering the extent of her injury. We stopped every five or six steps to let her rest. When we got close to the last gate, I ran ahead and turned the truck around, backing right up to the gate so Cinnamon could just walk right up the ramp into the trailer.

"I don't know how this is going to go," Reggie said. "She hasn't been on a trailer in a long time."

"No worries," I said. "Dr. R. can clicker train anything in five minutes. We'll get her on there. A few treats and some patience will do it every time."

He didn't look convinced, but to everyone's amazement, Cinnamon walked up the ramp without ever breaking stride.

"Well, how about that?" I said with a laugh. "It's like she's done it a thousand times."

"Well, she was a polo horse before we got her," Sadie said. "She probably *has* done it a thousand times."

I closed the trailer doors and turned to shake hands with Sadie and Reggie. "I'm going to get moving. It's a slow drive out to the main road. Don't worry about Cinnamon, she's in the best of care."

"Thank you for doing this," Sadie said. "I didn't know what we were going to do."

"You're very welcome. Enjoy your conference. I'll see you next week."

I jumped in the truck and slowly pulled out of the yard. Dr. Russel was finishing up the paperwork with them when I left, but it didn't take long for her to catch up with me on the winding road.

Once we got to the clinic, the team sprang into action. They thoroughly cleaned Cinnamon's wound, double checking that nothing vital had been damaged. It was difficult to see clearly, as the hole inside the muscle was much larger than the hole in the skin. The bull's horn was curved, and once it penetrated the skin, it went in and up, ripping its way through the muscle.

Dr. Russel set to stitching, starting deep inside the muscle.

"Can stitches really hold all that muscle together?" I asked.

"Sort of. I'm going to do it in three layers. Some of them will probably break, but it will be enough to hold it until it can get going on its own."

Once the muscle was stitched up, she located the bottom of the injury inside the shoulder and cut a small slice through the skin. This was about six inches below the tear where the horn had gone in. They inserted a drain through the bottom hole and fed it in until it came out the top, then sutured it in place. This is a long piece of plastic, similar to a straw, except not as rigid. Part of the healing process involves the body getting rid of damaged tissue and infection, which is expelled in serum and looks like gooey pus. It settles to the lowest part of the wound, and if there's no place for that nasty serum to go, then it becomes an abscess. Thus, we keep a spot open for it to drain out.

Stitching up the skin went quickly, and after a quick bath to clean all the blood that had run down her leg, she went into a stall for the weekend. We gathered at the door, watching as Cinnamon pulled mouthfuls of hay from the hay net.

"Well, she's got a good appetite," Cassie said. "That's always a good sign."

"For sure," Dr. Russel agreed, glancing at me. "Can you get her home on Monday?"

I pulled my phone out and checked my calendar. There was a time in my life when I didn't use a calendar, but I don't know how I managed. I guess I didn't have near as much going on in my life back then. "I can do it Monday afternoon. Does it matter to them what time?"

"I'm going to call them in a minute and let them know she's all patched up. They might be on a plane already, but I'll let you know as soon as I know."

"Perfect."

On Monday, I loaded Cinnamon and a big bag of medical supplies in the trailer and took her home. Reggie walked out of the barn and met me by the gate as I pulled up.

"Howdy. How's our girl?"

"She's probably not going to be playing polo for a few weeks, but she's pretty solid."

He let out a belly laugh and helped me drop the ramp on the trailer. "She ain't done more than eat in five years, so I reckon that's alright."

Cinnamon paused halfway down the ramp. She looked around for a moment and let out a whinny before hobbling the rest of the way down the ramp.

"Sounds like she's happy to be home," I said, handing Reggie the lead rope. "I'll grab the goody bag."

Reggie put Cinnamon in a stall and hung her halter on a peg beside the door. I handed him the bag.

"Dr. Russel wrote out all the care instructions for you here, so you don't have to try to remember everything she said on the phone. I'm sure you'll have some questions once you start doing all the stuff, so don't hesitate to call her. She's great about talking people through this stuff."

Reggie glanced over the papers. "Yeah, we've never had to do anything like this."

"Like I said, don't hesitate to call or text. If you don't get her, leave a message. She'll call you back."

He stuck out his hand. "I sure appreciate you all. This whole thing has been something else."

I shook his hand with a grin. "I'm sure it has. You might cut the points off your bulls horns, save yourself some trouble down the road."

He nodded. "Should've done it a long time ago."

The winding road back out to the highway wasn't so bad, now that I'd done it a few times. Reggie's intention to dull the horns on his bulls made me think about all the little projects that I've been putting off. Maybe this was a good time to get a few of those things done, at least the ones that could cause problems if left undone too long. As I drove down our long driveway, a tree branch scraped across the top of the trailer. Trimming that was probably a good place to start.

Chapter 3

What You Don't Know Can Hurt You

THERE'S A FINE LINE BETWEEN making observations and judging people, and I sometimes find myself crossing it. This usually happens when people do things that seem blatantly stupid regarding their horses. When I take a moment to examine my thought process and figure out why I arrived at that conclusion, it's almost always because I'm making assumptions. What assumptions? I assume that everyone who has a horse knows certain things about horses, and is therefore making an informed decision to do something ridiculous.

The truth is, lots of people know lots of things about horses, and nobody knows everything. If there were a thousand things that you could possibly know about horses, I would say the average horse owner knows about a hundred. Equine veterinarians probably know about five hundred. Then there are all kinds of experts that aren't veterinarians, like geneticists, behaviorists, professors, and so on. They also probably know five hundred, but it's a different five hundred than the vets. And each one hundred things that owners have is different from one person to the next. So, for me to assume that someone knows something specific just because they have a horse is just poor logic on my part, and not fair to that person.

Having said all that, this story is about a horse who became a victim of ignorance and happenstance. I don't want you to jump to the same conclusion that I did, nor do I want you to think that I'm publicly flogging someone for their ignorance. I'm telling this story to share knowledge and hopefully save some other horse from going through this experience.

One Saturday evening, which is when all emergencies seem to happen, Erica and I were returning home from treating a colic. It was a mild gas colic, and Erica was confident that it would be fine with our treatment of drugs and fluids. I had just turned on to our driveway when her phone rang.

"Hello, Dr. Lacher."

Since we had been listening to a podcast over the Bluetooth connection, the call came over the vehicle's speakers, and I got to hear the whole thing.

"Yes, I think something's wrong with my horse. He's acting really strange."

I stopped the truck. If we were going to see this horse, there was no point in driving down our very long dirt road. Erica opened her laptop.

"Okay, what's he doing?"

"He's just standing in one spot, kind of weaving around.

His head's down like he's trying to graze, but he's not eating anything. It's almost like he's about to fall down, or something."

"That doesn't sound good. How long has it been since he was last vaccinated?"

There was a pause. "You mean like getting a shot, or something?"

"Yeah, his Eastern and Western Encephalitis, West Nile, all those vaccines."

"He's never had any shots. He's never been sick or anything, so we've never needed a vet before."

This is the part where I started getting judgmental, but Erica rolled right on like the professional she is. "How old is he?"

"He's two and a half."

"It sounds like he's got some neurological behavior, which is probably encephalitis, and he definitely needs to be seen. Where are you located?"

While she gave Erica an address outside of Lake City, which is about forty-five minutes north of us, I got the truck turned around and headed down the road. It was going to be a late night.

"Do you think I need to get his mama out of this pasture? Is it from a poison weed, or something?"

"No, it's a mosquito-borne virus. Horses get it from mosquito bites. She's as safe there as she would be anywhere else."

"Oh, okay. I didn't want her getting it, too."

"We're about an hour away, maybe less," Erica said. "We'll be there as soon as we can."

Once they hung up, I let my frustrations out. "So, they're breeding, but they've never heard of vaccinating their horses?"

Erica sighed. "I know. It sounds impossible, right?"

It did sound impossible. Between our monthly seminars at the clinic, the podcast that Erica and I record twice a month, the weekly blog that I edit, and just being around the vet clinic all the time, I have endless amounts of horse knowledge coming at me every day. Therein lies my confirmation bias.

"I guess if she's never seen a veterinarian, and she doesn't look for horse care stuff online, she might not know," I grudgingly admitted. "There's not much excuse for it in the information age, though."

"She might not have internet," Erica said. "Lots of people don't, especially out in the boondocks around here. It's not even available in a lot of places."

I knew I was guilty of assuming that she had the same resources and opportunities for horse knowledge as I did, which is ridiculous. That realization made me feel embarrassed for jumping to conclusions, but I was glad I worked it out before we got there. Not that I would have treated her any differently, because I still believe in building relationships, but I would have felt worse afterwards. This whole holding myself to higher standards thing is tough sometimes.

It was full dark by the time we made the last turn. We were in a rural area with more trailers than houses. I crept down the road as the mailbox numbers got close. She'd said they were out in a field, and spotting them from the road could be difficult.

"There's the mailbox," Erica said. Her long-range night vision is way better than mine.

"The pasture was before the house, right?"

"Right."

I pulled into the driveway and turned around. There was no traffic out here, so I turned the headlights on bright and rolled back up the road at ten miles an hour. The weeds were grown up through the fence, and we could only see into the field intermittently at best.

"There," Erica said, pointing. "Headlights coming this way. Look for a gate."

The headlights bounced and twisted, alternately shining up in the air and disappearing. I began to get nervous about driving across there. Our vet truck was an SUV, and it didn't have four-wheel drive. With all the rain we'd been getting, the prospect of getting stuck in a field was grim, but very real. At last we spotted a gate and a little-used road leading away from the pavement into the darkness. I turned in and waited for the distant vehicle to arrive.

While we waited, I tried to brush up on my encephalitis knowledge. "If this really is an encephalitis case, there's not much we can do besides euthanize, right?"

"Pretty much," Erica said. "We can take it to the clinic and try to support it, but EEE cases are almost always fatal if they're not vaccinated. If it's West Nile, we might have a shot at saving it. It depends on a lot of things."

"How can you tell the difference?" I asked. "The only way to know exactly what it is, is to send blood to a lab, right?"

"Yeah, but there are some telling signs. Encephalitis usually has a fever of 105 or so, and West Nile is more like 102, for one thing."

"I see."

The bouncing headlights pulled up to the gate, and I hopped out to stand in the light. It's a little bit scary running around out here in the dark, and I didn't want to get shot at by someone misunderstanding our intentions. A man climbed out of the truck and walked over to the gate.

"Howdy," I called, walking up to the gate. "I'm Justin, with Springhill Equine Veterinary Clinic. Have you got a sick horse?"

"Jim." He nodded his head. He looked to be in his early thirties with dark hair and a stubble beard. "You can follow me over to the horse. Try to stay in my tracks, it's a little wet out there."

"Will do." I walked back to the vet truck as he opened the gate.

The pasture was more than a little wet as far as I was concerned. In some places the ground disappeared altogether, as if we were driving across a lake. I couldn't even see the road once we left the gate, and I stayed glued to his bumper as we sloshed across the marshy field.

"This place is Mecca for mosquitos," I said, trying to distract myself from the terror of getting stuck. "You can see them in the headlights. I hope we've got some bug spray."

Erica reached into the cubby on her door and produced a squirt bottle. "Got you covered."

We veered around a few trees, the seatbelts preventing our heads from crashing into the roof as we hit holes and rocks. It was too rough to go this fast, but too muddy to go any slower: the perfect paradox.

At last the truck in front of us turned to the right and climbed onto higher ground. We could see some people standing with two horses up ahead. The ground was drier here, and I pulled up beside the truck as he parked to add additional light to the situation. Erica stepped out and quickly sprayed herself with bug spray, then tossed the bottle to me and disappeared behind the vet truck. I joined her a moment later.

"What all do we need?" I asked, using the light on my phone to Illuminate the vet box. We were immediately swarmed by mosquitos, and I waved them away from my face. "Besides more bug spray."

"Just stethoscope and thermometer for starters. Let's go check it out."

We walked around the truck and approached the group. An elderly man stood to one side, his faded plaid shirt nearly matching my own. A young woman stood beside the horse with a baby on her hip. Her hair was dark like her husband's, as was the toddler's.

There was no question about which horse was sick. The mare was off to one side, grazing on the tall grass. The other horse stood with his head between his knees, swaying like he'd been heavily sedated. Erica walked up and shook hands with the woman.

"Hi, I'm Dr. Lacher."

"I'm Casey," she said. "This is Cash."

"Let's see what's going on." Erica put her stethoscope on and listened to Cash's heart and his breathing, then went around back and took his temperature. She ran her hands over him briefly, then lifted his head up a bit and checked his gums and his eyes.

"He's got a pretty high fever," she said, letting his head droop back down. "I'll have to do a blood test to confirm it, but he presents like a classic encephalitis case." She waved the bugs away from her ears. "It's a really nasty virus. I wish I had better news for you, but there's not much we can do for him."

Casey bit her lip and turned away, and her husband spoke up. "Is it fatal?"

Erica nodded. "If we don't do anything, he'll go down tonight or tomorrow, and he won't be able to get back up. After that they start having seizures, and then they die. It's a horrible way to go."

Casey burst into tears, which caused the baby to start crying, too. "Is there something you can do?"

Erica patted Cash on the neck with a sad smile. "We could get him to our clinic and put him on some anti-inflammatory drugs and a lot of fluids, and basically support him as well as we can, but his immune system has to fight this off. Once they get to this point, they almost never recover, and we'd just be spending a lot of money for nothing. I'm really sorry, Casey. No one wants to get this news about their pony, and I hate giving it, but the best thing we can do is put him out of his misery."

Casey turned and buried her face in her husband's chest. The baby girl, who had stopped crying briefly, looked around in surprise, and started crying again. If it hadn't been so sad, I would have laughed. She clearly had no idea what she was crying about, but she was showing solidarity with her mom. Her tears sparkled like diamonds in the headlights.

I had forgotten the old man was there, and I jumped when he stepped up into the light beside them and put a hand on the younger man's shoulder. Side by side, it was clear they were father and son. The square jaw, the paunch, the eyes, it was all there.

"Best let her put him to sleep," he said. "No need to make him suffer."

"But he's my bu-baby," Casey gasped, her chest heaving. "I just started training him."

"I know, baby, I know." Jim wrapped his arms around her and the baby, and the four of them stood there together.

"I didn't even knu-know about the vac-vaccines," she said. "I killed my baby!"

"No, baby, don't say that," he said, rubbing her head. "Don't do that to yourself. You know you didn't kill him."

Part of me agreed with her, that she did kill him by not learning what she needed to know before she got a horse. That wasn't fair, because you don't know what you don't know. A lot of people grow up in a culture where no one in their sphere uses a veterinarian. Hell, I grew up that way. None of my childhood dogs ever saw a vet, or got a vaccine or a heartworm preventative. I didn't even know that was a thing until I was an adult. Who was I to throw stones at this poor family? It's funny how once you learn something, you think everyone else should know that, too. Or maybe it's just me that does that, I don't know.

"This is something that happens in nature," Erica said. "It's a tragedy, and it's going to hurt, but don't rub salt on it. I'm sure you've been a good mom for him."

I felt terrible for Cash. Viruses are a cruel, heartless thing, destroying everything they touch. I couldn't even guess at how many millions of animals and people have been killed by them over the course of time. Now that I've learned more about viruses and how they function, I find the fact that we've figured out how to successfully vaccinate against a few of them to be amazing.

The old man patted them both before stepping back. "I'll go get the tractor. We'll have to bury him." He disappeared into the darkness.

"Okay," Casey said, wiping her nose on her sleeve. She kissed the baby, who had stopped crying again. "I guess we have to do this, then. How does it work?"

Erica stepped up beside Cash. "It's really fast and painless. I'm going to give him a shot, and he's basically going to fall asleep and not wake up. You don't have to be here for it if you don't want to."

"Why don't you go up to the house?" Jim said. "Me and

daddy will take care of it. You need to get the baby out of these mosquitos, anyway. She's getting eat up."

Casey nodded and scrubbed her face on her shoulder. "Alright. Give me the flashlight."

Once they were gone, we got to work. "Which way are you going to do it?" I asked. We'd recently learned a new technique for euthanizing horses that were going to be buried. It took a bit longer, but the drugs involved wouldn't pollute the groundwater the way phenobarbital does, and as a Save The Planet kind of guy, I liked the idea a lot.

"We'll use the new way," Erica said. "I'll get it pulled up if you'll get the clippers and the catheter."

Jim stood by Cash, trying to pet him as he swayed. Cash's knees were wobbly, and I was concerned that he might go down before we could get this done. If that happened, this would get a hundred times more dangerous. I grabbed the hanging lead rope and lifted his head up.

"Is this where you want to do it?" Erica asked.

Jim looked around. "Yeah, I guess. Daddy can move him with the tractor if we need to."

"Okay, we're going to do this quick before he crashes." Jim stepped back out of the way. It took both of my hands to hold Cash's head up while Erica placed the catheter. Once it was in, she administered the shots, jamming the plungers down as fast as she could.

Really sick horses can take longer to go, and Cash was in bad shape. I was glad Casey had decided to leave. Cash hit the ground hard, and his legs spasmed for a minute before falling still. He let out a final cough, and it was over.

I put the stuff away as Erica typed up the bill. Jim came over with a credit card as she was finishing up. "What's the damages?"

Erica handed him the bill, and his face fell. "$350, and a dead horse." He shook his head. "How much is vaccines?"

"About $75 twice a year," Erica said. "Occasionally, a vaccinated horse can still get the virus, but if we give the vaccine, the drug company pays for it to get treated, and they usually make a full recovery." She handed his card back with the receipt. "I'd recommend getting any other horses you've got vaccinated as soon as you can."

"Yep, we'll do that." He turned as a set of headlights appeared around the trees. "Here comes daddy. I'll guide you out to the gate as soon as he gets over here."

We shook hands and got in the truck. The ride out was just as rough as the ride in, and the cab was full of mosquitos, but we made it to the pavement without incident. It was a quiet ride home. Erica spent most of the time trying to kill all the mosquitos. I thought about Casey, and wondered how we might have reached her before tragedy struck. We try really hard to educate people with our free seminars, the podcast, and the weekly blog. Short of knocking on doors, I didn't know what else we could do to keep this kind of thing from happening. Even with that, it takes a tragedy to get some people's attention. That's what it took to get my attention all those years ago, after all. I once again resolved to avoid throwing stones and to try to find solutions instead. Keeping a positive attitude is hard work, but it's worth it at the end of the day.

Chapter 4

JUST HANGING OUT

ONE OF THE THINGS THAT ERICA AND I DO to contribute to our mission, which is to make the world a better place for horses, is produce a podcast called *Straight from the Horse Doctor's Mouth*. This is a great way to share Erica's knowledge with horse people all over the world, which they can then use to make the world a better place for their horse. I have learned a ton of stuff doing this, which is great since I came into the horse world so late in life.

It's funny how things happen in life that you can't really appreciate until much later. This podcast is one of those things. When I was in my early thirties, I started a band with three other guys. I was single then, which meant that I was the one with disposable income. As we wrote more songs and started to get our sound together, we decided to record our own album. As the one with the money, I bought a bunch of good audio equipment and turned my living room into a recording studio.

Flash forward ten years. The band has gone the way of the dodo bird (gone, but not forgotten!) but I still have all this equipment. So, we use the PA system at our monthly seminars, and we use the recording equipment to produce our podcast. It's funny, because I tried really hard to sell all that stuff before I moved to Florida and married Erica. I never thought I'd need it again. Fortunately, I couldn't find any buyers who were willing to pay my prices, so I still have almost all of it, and it gets used all the time. Who knew?

One Saturday morning I was setting up the studio, getting ready to record our next episode. It would be great if I could leave everything set up all the time, but with five cats running around, that's just not a good plan. I rolled out the mic cables, got the mixer set up, and fired up the recorder. Erica sat down in her chair and adjusted her notes as I tested the audio levels.

"Testing, testing." I moved the dial up a bit more. "Testing."

"I can't hear you," Erica said.

"That's because you don't have your headphones on." I pointed to the table beside her chair.

"Oh. Duh." She laughed and grabbed the phones, sliding them over her ears. "I guess that would probably help."

"Can you hear me now?"

"There we go!" She adjusted her notes on the music stand and took a sip of coffee. "How do I sound?"

"Fabulous." I got my music stand in place and poised my finger over the record button. "Ready?"

Two things happen at this point almost every time we

try to record a podcast. First, one of the cats, usually Ari, will come in and jump on Erica's lap and start rubbing his head on the microphone. Second, the dog will come racing in with a squeaker toy, ready to play and make tons of noise. Podcasting is a family event around here. Right on cue, Mimi came flying in with Mr. Duck in tow. It took a minute of wrestling, but I managed to get Mr. Duck away from her and remove her collar.

"I promise we'll play as soon as I get done," I said, ruffling her ears. Mimi is a rescue Shih Tzu, and probably one of my top three favorite critters on the planet.

"Come on, get it over with." Erica's voice in my headphones caused me to glance over just as the yellow cat leaped into her lap.

"Okay, I think we're really ready this time," I said. Erica nodded, and I pressed record. "Hello everybody, and welcome to the podcast. I am your host, Justin Long, and I'm here with the most famous horse doctor in all of podcasting, Dr. Erica Lacher. Hello, Dr. Lacher."

"Hello, Justin Long."

We start the podcast the same way every time. It keeps the beginning smooth and helps us get into the groove. Mimi began gnawing on my toe, which is also normal, and I settled into my seat.

"I'd like to thank everyone, wherever you are around the world, for joining us today. We've got people listening in over fifty countries now, which is just amazing to me... and it sounds like one of them is calling us right now." I hit the STOP button as Erica grabbed her phone. I knew better than to try to record a podcast when we're on call. It's just tempting fate!

"Address?" Erica grabbed a pen and jotted the information on the back of her show notes. "We'll be there in ten minutes.

Don't try to do anything. Keep everyone out of the stall. We're on the way."

I was already powering down the equipment by the time she hung up. "What do we have?"

"That was the sheriff's department. They've got a horse upside down in a stall with his rear foot stuck in the window bars."

I did a double take. "What? Really? How does that even happen? I mean, I can see a front foot-"

"Walk and talk," Erica said, pushing me towards the door. "Luckily, it's close by."

We raced down the stairs and jumped in the vet truck. Mimi stood at the top of the stairs, looking disappointed. I had recently shoveled a truckload of lime rock into the potholes, so our driveway was relatively smooth as we flew down it.

"Who calls the sheriff for something like this?" I asked. "I don't think that would even occur to me."

"Someone who doesn't have a veterinarian."

"Huh." I shook my head.

I'm going to climb up on my soapbox for a minute. If you have a horse, you should have a veterinarian. That doesn't mean that you do a Google search and pick a name that you'll call if you ever have an emergency. That means you have a veterinarian who sees your horse at least once a year, preferably twice. Having a horse is a 24/7 lifestyle, and having a relationship with a veterinarian who knows you, and knows your horses, should be part of that lifestyle. If an emergency happens, you'll already have an appropriate and reliable response team in place. The fact that you've never had an emergency before is in no way a guarantee that you won't have one in the future, and you shouldn't gamble with your horse's well-being. Okay, I'm climbing off my soapbox now.

Erica directed me around a few corners, and we pulled up a long, wooded drive. As we passed a bend in the road, a large house came into view. There were flowers everywhere, and as we pulled into the yard, a blue heeler came racing around the house to meet us. I angled to the left, following the tires tracks in the dew-wet grass.

Behind the house, two sheriff's department SUVs sat parked in front of a small brown wooden barn. Ivy climbed a trellis to the tin roof on one side, and light poured out the concrete aisleway through the open door. Erica was out of the truck before I even had it in park, and we ran inside.

Two older women stood beside a stall door, peering through it. We could hear a horse blowing and breathing heavily inside. The women turned as we came in, and the taller one stepped forward.

"He's in here. Can you do something?"

"Well, let's see what we've got," Erica said. "I'm Dr. Lacher, by the way. This is my husband, Justin."

"I'm Jill Brown, just a friend helping out. Cassandra is very upset, as you can imagine."

I glanced at the other woman. Her short grey hair was immaculate, and her sleeveless shirt showed arms that clearly spent a fair amount of time in the gym. She blew her nose into a wrinkled tissue, her red-rimmed eyes saying everything that needed to be said.

The horse lay on his back in the stall. His left hind hoof was jammed through the vertical bars that separated the top half of his stall from the next. His front legs and head were flopped over to one side, and his black coat was shiny with sweat. The two sheriff's deputies were in the adjoining stall. As we took in the scene, one of them came out into the aisle.

"Hey, Dr. Lacher. You made way better time than we did." He stuck his hand out with a grin.

"I was probably closer than you were," Erica said, giving his hand a quick shake. "I assume you've tried prying the bars apart?"

"Yep, they're not budging, and the way he keeps thrashing, I'm afraid he's going to tear his leg off."

I cringed as Cassandra burst into tears at the statement. I probably shouldn't judge a cop for his bedside manner, but he was clearly oblivious of his impact on others. I glanced up at the top of the stall wall. It was a common construction method for stalls. The bottom half was wood planks, and the top half was aluminum poles placed about four inches apart. An aluminum beam ran across the top and bottom, screwed to the wooden frame, and the upright poles were seated through holes in the beams.

"I think we're going to have to pull the top beam off to separate the bars," I said. "Do you think we can sedate him like that?"

Erica let out a deep breath. This was an extremely dangerous situation, and I could sense that she was weighing the odds. The safest thing for us would be to take it apart without sedating the horse or going in the stall at all. That wouldn't be the safest thing for the horse, though, as he was likely to panic if we start taking the wall apart while he was lying in a vulnerable position. It was a tough spot.

"We're going to have to shoot some radiographs once we get him out of there," she said. "I'm going to need him awake to really see how bad he's hurt himself. Let's try to do a light sedation, just enough to calm him down and get him out of there."

"What do you want us to do?" the deputy asked.

"Find a ladder and a drill and get ready to unscrew that top rail once I give you the go ahead. We'll give him a shot. I don't want anybody inside that stall except me. It's too dangerous with the position he's in."

"I've got tools," Cassandra said. "Do whatever you need to do. I don't care if you tear it up, we've got to get him out of there."

"Don't worry, we'll get him out." I gave her a reassuring smile and hoped the deputy didn't say anything to send her off the deep end again.

Jill took the deputies to find tools, and we went back out to the truck. Erica pulled up a syringe of sedation.

"Do you want me to hold his head down for you?" I asked.

"No, I don't want you getting kicked," she said around the needle cap between her teeth.

I was secretly relieved. The idea of going in there with a horse in distress was terrifying. He might have one leg stuck, but the other three could go pretty much anywhere faster than we could react.

We went back inside. The deputies had two step ladders and were waiting down the aisle to avoid upsetting the horse.

Erica stopped beside Jill. "Is there a helmet here I can borrow?"

Jill glanced at Cassandra, who nodded. "Sure, in the tack room."

Jill and Erica disappeared into the room beside the front door. I glanced in the stall, my heart going out to the poor horse. His nostrils flared with each breath, and his visible eye rolled up to look at me. "Hold tight, buddy," I whispered. "We're going to get you out of there."

Erica returned a moment later with a black riding helmet on. I would have preferred that she have something more akin to a pro football player's helmet and pads, but time was of the essence, and this was what we had.

"What's his name?" Erica asked.

"Coal," Jill said. "His registered name is Black Diamond, but his barn name is Coal."

"Got it. Okay, Coal, I'm coming in." She carefully slid the stall door open.

It was totally unnecessary for me to say anything as she walked in the stall, but I couldn't help myself. "Be careful. I love you."

She was focused on her task and didn't respond, but I knew she heard me. I held my breath as she crossed the stall, hugging the wall. She whispered soothing sounds as she squatted down and duck-walked to his head, ready to lunge away if he struck out. I could feel my pulse pounding in my neck, my wrists, and my temples. Everything stood out to me, the sound of the ceiling fan spinning overhead, the shaft of sunlight peeking in the window on the far wall, the smell of horse poop and fresh bedding. If I hadn't been so terrified for Erica, I probably would have been lost in the moment of surrealism.

Erica crept closer, reaching out with one hand. She continued to talk to the horse, and he lay still, watching her. After rubbing his muzzle for a minute, she worked her way behind his head. He stayed flopped over on his side, which I attributed to my will power, and Erica began rubbing his neck. She pinched him a few times, and when he didn't react, she slipped the syringe out of her pocket.

"Here we go, Coal. Just a quick poke, and you'll feel way better. Just go easy." She pulled the cap off the needle, put her thumb over his vein, and expertly slid the needle in and depressed the plunger. Coal didn't even twitch.

I let out a breath that I didn't know I was holding as Erica moved slowly back to the corner, out of reach. We waited for a few long minutes in silence, watching Coal, and waiting for the drugs to take effect. He finally let out a deep sigh, and visibly relaxed. Erica made her way back out of the stall.

"Okay, let's get the bar off. Try to be as quiet as possible, and don't make sudden moves. He's sedated, but he's still very much awake."

The deputies nodded and hurried up the far side of the aisle with the ladders to the next stall. I followed them in to be an extra set of hands. There were approximately ten thousand screws holding the upper bar to the rafter joist. The deputies handed them down to me as they pulled them out, and I put them in the empty water bucket on the wall, making sure I didn't drop a single screw. The last thing we needed was for the horse that lived in this stall to step on one, or roll on it and get punctured.

When they got down to the last two screws, they paused to make a plan.

"Okay," Deputy Henderson said. "I think it's going to pull everything towards his stall when we get these screws out. He's got some weight on it. Hopefully his foot pops out as soon as we lift the top bar off, but if it doesn't, we need to make sure it all doesn't go crashing in on him."

"How about you guys hold the bars on the ends, and I'll hold the ones around his leg. I think you can just drop the top bar as soon as it's off. There's bedding in here. If his foot doesn't come out, I'll pull the bar out while you guys keep the rest of it standing up." I glanced at them for confirmation, and they nodded.

"Just be careful on the ladder," Henderson said to his partner. "If it starts to pull you over, let go."

"Got it."

We all got in position. Deputy Henderson pulled the screw on his end first, sliding it in his pocket as he handed the drill to Davis. The whole structure bowed in, and Henderson quickly grabbed the end bars to steady it. I put a hand on each of the poles bracing Coal's hoof.

"Ready?"

"Let's do it."

Davis held a pole with one hand and pulled the final screw with the other. The bars leaned in more as Davis fumbled with the screw before dropping it and the drill to the floor to grab the other bar.

"We'll find it later," I said, straining to keep the whole thing from leaning in and tearing the bottom screws out of the wall, or bending the bars. "Let's lean it in a bit more and slide the top off."

We carefully let the whole thing lean in towards Coal a bit more, until the top bar was away from the board above it. Coal jerked his leg as the pressure on it changed, nearly ripping the whole thing out of our grasp.

"Hold it!" Henderson grunted. "I'll try to get the bar off."

He let go of the bar with one hand and tried to slide the top rail off the poles. His end came up, but it was too long for him to have enough leverage to get the whole thing.

"I got it," Davis said. "Grab on."

Henderson let go of the rail and grabbed the bar again. The muscles in my shoulders and neck were starting to burn. It was an awkward angle for me, holding that much weight at head level, but at least I had the luxury of bracing my hip on the lower wall. I wasn't sure how the deputies were managing up on the ladders. Their backs had to be on fire.

Davis carefully let go with one hand, making sure that we had it before he began working the top rail off on his end. As soon as it came off the two poles I was holding, I spread them to the sides as far as they would go. Coal's hoof slid down lower instead of coming out, and he jerked again, nearly tearing the bars out of my grasp.

I let go of the pole on my left, grabbing the one on the right with both hands. The pressure against it was enormous, but I twisted it as I lifted, trying to gain every edge I could. It moved a fraction. I was afraid my neck was going to cramp, which would be really bad, and my sweaty hands started to slide on the bar. I gripped it tighter and yanked with all my might. At last the pole popped out of the base bar, and I fell over backwards.

Coal let out a deafening whinny as I climbed to my feet. He might have been sedated, but he was ecstatic to have his foot back. I stuck the pole back in the base bar.

"Let's get this thing back together," Henderson said.

I handed the top rail up to him and dug around in the bedding until I found the screw and the drill. Putting all the bars back into the holes in the rail proved to be the hardest part of the whole operation. Getting the first few in wasn't bad, but then they would fall back out as we tried to get the next few in.

"Let's pull the whole thing over to this side of the wall," I suggested. "Then we can let it lean all the way, and just work the top rail down over the whole thing at once."

"Huh." Davis climbed down off his ladder. "Sounds good to me."

Coal was still down in his stall. I've worked on enough vehicles to know how my arm feels after being over my head for a few minutes. His whole leg had to be completely numb by now, and he was going to have a world-class case of the tingles soon.

We moved the ladders and pulled all the bars over to this side of the wall. It only took a few minutes of wrestling with it to get the top rail back on, and they quickly screwed it all back in place. I could see Erica over at the stall door. It looked like she was trying to keep Cassandra from rushing into the stall. It was an understandable urge, to be sure, but Coal wasn't ready for visitors just yet. Between the sedation and his numb leg, he could hurt someone without intending to. I made my way back around to Erica.

"Let's get the x-ray in here," she said. "Once he's able to stand, we need to see what kind of shape that leg is in.

I followed her out to the truck. I wasn't sure if I could even carry the digital x-ray machine. It comes in two suitcases, and it's not light. My shoulders and neck were still burning from my exertion, but I couldn't quit now. I unloaded the cases with a groan and carried them inside. On a normal day, I'd have put both lead aprons on too, just to save myself a trip back to the truck, but I decided that walking twice would be easier than carrying all that at once.

Jill turned as we came back to the stall. "He just tried to get up, but he didn't make it."

Erica nodded. "Okay. It's probably going to take a while before he can do it."

We got the x-ray unpacked and plugged in while we waited. Deputy Davis left, and Henderson filled out his incident report. I could imagine the eyebrows that would get raised by the people who process these things at the sheriff's department. This had to be unusual for them!

"Alright, I think you guys have things under control here,"

Henderson said, glancing through the stall door at Coal. "I'm going to get out of here. And tell Coal I said to behave, no more shenanigans."

Cassandra gave him a hug. "Thank you so much for coming. I just didn't know what to do."

"Next time, call the vet first," he said, patting her shoulder. "She's got the drugs."

Cassandra sniffled and tried to smile. "Yes, sir. But there better not be a next time. Once in a lifetime is plenty."

We all laughed. It's crazy how stressful something like this can be. I have to remind myself all the time that even though I see horses doing crazy things all the time, it's usually a first for the horse owners, and it's terrifying to see your horse in a bad predicament.

It took nearly an hour for Coal to stand up. Once he was safely upright, we let him stand for a bit longer. At first, he held the leg up in the air, not putting any weight on it. Gradually, it dropped to the floor.

"Okay, let's get a halter on him," Erica said. "I'll check him out, and then we'll try to get some radiographs."

"It's right here," Jill said, handing me a halter. I stepped into the stall.

Coal was facing away from the door, still in the same spot as when he stood up. I glanced over at the wall where his foot had been stuck, and tried to imagine how he had managed to do it. From a physics perspective, it was a crazy acrobatic move to buck and kick that high with enough force to get his hoof through the bars, and to then flip over on his back. I couldn't figure out how he got his other rear leg clear without breaking his hip. My brain threatened to cramp, so I stopped trying to figure it out and slid the halter over his nose.

"Hey, buddy, we're going to check you out." I rubbed his neck as Erica came in and began her exam.

"Watch that he doesn't bite you," Cassandra said. "He's not always well-behaved."

"Okay," I said. "Thanks for the heads up." Despite the number of horses I've met on emergencies, I haven't been bitten by one yet, though I've had some close calls. I'm sure it will happen eventually.

Erica picked up his sore leg and flexed it up and down, back and forth, watching closely for a pain response. Coal was a perfect gentleman, and didn't show any signs of pain. She set his foot down and grabbed his tail, pulling him towards her. It took a minute, but he finally let out a sigh and put his weight on the leg.

"That's promising," Erica said. "So far, so good. Let's shoot some images of those joints and double check everything."

"You think he's okay?" Cassandra asked. A fresh tear ran down her cheek.

"Well, he's going to be sore, for sure, but so far, it doesn't look like he did anything major."

Erica pulled her lead apron on and grabbed the x-ray generator. I slid into my own apron and pulled the plate out of the case, carefully spooling out the cable to where no one, especially Coal, would step on it or trip over it. Everything about the digital x-ray is expensive.

"Alright, we'll start low and work our way around and up." Erica positioned the plate, and I did my best to hold it still. We shot a few different angles of his foot, then moved up and started over. My back was aching after a few minutes, but I gritted my teeth and tried to tough it out. It took nearly twenty minutes, but the higher we got, the less it hurt. At last, I was able to put the plate away, take off the apron, and stretch my back. Cassandra and Jill crowded around the screen as Erica began going through the images. She went through them slowly, explaining what she was looking for in each one.

"He hasn't shattered any bones, since he's willing to put weight on it, but there could still be fractures. I don't see anything so far, but we're watching for a thin dark line in here." She slowly advanced through the images. "We can't see up high on his leg or his hip. There's just too much mass to see through. Everything that we can see looks good, though."

Cassandra let out a sigh, and Jill put a hand on her shoulder.

Erica closed the last image and looked at Coal, shaking her head. "You're the luckiest horse in town, kiddo. I don't know how you managed that." She turned back to Cassandra and Jill. "He's going to be sore for a few days, but I think he'll probably be okay, as long as there aren't any fractures that we can't see. We'll keep him in the stall for a few days and put him on some bute for the pain, but he shouldn't need anything else. If he comes up lame, or stops putting weight on it, let me know so we can see what's going on."

"Oh, that's wonderful news," Cassandra said. Jill wrapped her arm around Cassandra's shoulders and gave her a squeeze.

I began packing up the stuff and carrying it back out to the vet truck as Erica typed up the care instructions and the bill. We gathered back in front of Coal's stall when we were finished.

"Here's everything written down, so you don't have to remember anything I said." Erica handed the paperwork to Cassandra. "My phone number is right at the top. You can call me, text me, send me videos, or whatever, all to that number. I'll call you tomorrow to check on him, and I'd like to stop in Monday and take a peek at him. If he's doing good at that point, we'll talk about turning him out."

"Of course, whatever we need to do." Cassandra looked down at her feet. "I realize I should have called you right away, now. The policeman was right. We probably would have had him out a lot sooner."

Erica shrugged with a wry grin. "Well, you don't know until you know, and now you know. That's horses."

Jill leaned in and shook Erica's hand. "Thank you for doing this. We're incredibly grateful for your help."

"You're welcome. We're here if you need us, 24/7."

By the time we got back home, I had completely forgotten what the podcast was going to be about. We took a few minutes to regroup and started again. It went smooth the second time, with no interruptions. I was grateful; not because we got the podcast done, but because I was too tired for any more major events like that one. One per day is plenty, trust me!

Chapter 5

GERALD AND THE RENTAL SHEEP

ERICA IS THE KIND OF PERSON WHO LOVES to try out new things. When something new comes on the market, she doesn't wait to see what other people think, she jumps right in if it's something she's interested in. For example, we built a static aerated compost system for our horse manure. There are a few people doing this, but the information online is sketchy at best, and we've had to figure it out as we go. It's way better for our pastures than spreading fresh, un-composted manure and bedding.

Once we got the compost system built, we managed to get our feed store to order cardboard bedding for our stalls. The idea was that it had no dust, unlike the pelletized pine bedding we were using, which is great for heaves horses as well as general cleanliness. Cardboard will also compost much faster than shavings, and since our compost system is designed around a 90-day cycle, that was a big deal for us. We've since moved on to hemp bedding. It has much less waste than cardboard, and it's new, and it makes Erica happy. You understand.

We have often joked about borrowing the neighbor's goats to eat the weeds down in our pastures. This was always a joke and only a joke, because goats look at things like fences and trucks as obstacles to be overcome, challenges to master, mountains to climb. So, the day Erica made her announcement, I was surprised, to say the least.

"We're getting some sheep."

I turned away from the computer screen, assuming I'd misunderstood her. "Say again?"

"We're getting some sheep. For the weeds."

"I thought we decided that was a bad idea."

"No, we decided goats were a bad idea. Sheep are different."

I turned back to the computer and saved my work. It sounded like the decision had already been made, but this could still be a long discussion, and I don't like to take chances with the bookkeeping.

"How much is this going to cost?" I asked. It seemed like a reasonable place to start.

The smug grin on Erica's face told me she was already two steps ahead of me. "Nothing."

My eyebrows shot up. "Nothing? Did you accept sheep as payment for veterinary services?"

She laughed, and I relaxed. "No, we're borrowing them. They can go back home any time."

My first reaction was to find a way to prevent this from happening. My second reaction was to override the first reaction before it got me in trouble. I've found this mantra to be true for me: *First thoughts are for entertainment purposes only.* I took a deep breath and slowly let it out.

"Okay, so we're getting some rental sheep. How is this going to work?"

Erica began unloading her lunch pail as she talked. Her face was glowing, and I knew she was excited about this. "I think we have to put them in with the donkeys, just for their safety. Ralph says they don't really eat grass, and they'll eat around horse poop, which the horses won't do. We just put them out there, and in a month or two, we'll move everybody to another pasture, and just rotate them around until the weeds are all gone."

Hannah Banana and Pet, our donkeys, were going to be thrilled. I don't know why I was so against the idea, and I did my best to shake it off. I certainly didn't want to ruin Erica's mood with my pessimism. I resolved to accept the idea, and even try to embrace it.

"Okay, so what do we need to do to prepare? I assume they're about the same as goats, right?"

She shook her head. "Nope, Ralph says he doesn't have any problems with them breaking out. They'll strip an area clean, tree leaves and all, up to three feet off the ground. We just have to make sure we block off the garden if we let them out around the house."

We talked more about it over dinner, and by the time we went to bed, I was more or less okay with the idea. When they arrived a few days later, I still had some trepidation, but I hid it as best as I could. Ralph pulled a long stock trailer up our driveway and around back to the rear pastures. Mimi and Rachel, the dogs, didn't know what to think about the sounds and smells coming from the trailer, but they were extremely curious about it. I had to shoo them out of the way as Ralph backed up to the gate.

"Howdy!" Ralph hopped out of his truck and walked towards us. He was very spry and energetic for a man in his late seventies. I guess you have to be if you're going to keep raising cows and sheep at that age, and he has a bunch of both. His bald head gleamed in the sunshine.

"Hi, Ralph," Erica said. She was grinning from ear to ear. "The whole crew is here to welcome the sheep."

Behind us, both donkeys and both horses were lined up at the gate, and the dogs were running up and down the trailer sniffing things.

"It looks that way," Ralph chuckled. "Aw, heck, I forgot my list. Hang on a minute." He turned and hurried back to the cab of the truck, talking over his shoulder. "I wrote down the ear tag numbers on them when I put them on, but I want to double check them. It's hard to see when they're milling around in a bunch."

He returned a moment later with a yellow legal pad.

"Okay," I said. "What's the best way to do this?"

He released the latch on the trailer door. "One of you can get in the trailer and push them out. I'll check their tag number as they come out."

I nodded. "Okie dokie. Let me get the girls back away from the gate." I began shooing the horses and donkeys away, but they wouldn't go far. I picked up a stick and waved it, and Stitches and Jackie finally wandered off to the hay feeder. Hannah Banana and Pet stood their ground.

"Don't you two cause any trouble," I said sternly. "I know how you are, especially you, Hannah." I gave them a mock glare and went back to the gate, opening it up wide. The trailer filled all but a foot of the space, so I wasn't too worried about anyone escaping.

"Alright," I said. "I think we're ready. I'll get in the trailer and push them this way."

"No, I got it," Erica said. "I can stand up in there. You'd be hunched over." She's very thoughtful like that, and I gratefully agreed.

Ralph slid a panel open on the door, which I thought was pretty nifty. Instead of having to open the whole back end, we had a narrow opening so we could control the flow of exiting sheep.

"How many do we have?" I asked, peering into the dark interior. Erica climbed through the gap, cutting off my view.

"Eighteen," Ralph said. "Alright Dr. Lacher, you'll probably have to shove them out the door, they ain't gonna be too excited about getting off in a strange place."

"Got it." Erica's voice was drowned out by the bleating of sheep and stomping feet as she moved past them to the other end of the trailer.

The metal panels inside rattled like thunder as the sheep shuffled around. Hannah Banana walked past me and stuck her head inside the trailer, and I jumped.

"Damnit, I thought we talked about this." I swatted her on the rump, and she backed up a few steps. I grabbed her under the jaw and led her towards the hay feeder. "You can't be in the middle of this, or we'll never get the sheep off the trailer." It was clear that my job was going to be keeping the donkeys back away from the action.

Another thunder of rattling panels and a cry from Ralph caused me to spin around. Ralph lay on the ground, bear-hugging a sheep. Beside them, a line of sheep jumped out of the trailer like they were springing over a ten-foot wall and raced down the fence line. I let go of Hannah and ran over to help Ralph.

"Are you okay?"

"Grab the sheep," he grunted. I realized that from his vantage point, he couldn't see that the rest of the sheep had already exited stage left. I grabbed the sheep, lifting it off his chest, and Erica jumped down and helped him sit up.

"The rascal caught me before I was ready," he said, wiping sheep slobber off his glasses with a handkerchief.

Erica was looking him over. "Are you hurt?"

He shook his head. "Nah, just my pride. I might need a hand up, though."

I looked at the ear tag on the sheep I was holding before letting it go and grabbing his hand. "Well, we know we've got 655, anyway."

We got Ralph to his feet, and he looked out at the sheep. They were in a tight bunch about twenty feet away, staring at the donkeys. "Well, I reckon we'll check numbers in a few weeks. I'll have to come over and deworm them pretty soon. We'll do it then."

"Sounds like a good plan." I picked up his legal pad and tried to brush the dirt off. It was covered in poopy hoof prints.

Once he caught his breath and we were sure he was okay, we helped him close the trailer up. I was impressed that he took the fall so well, especially with a seventy-pound sheep on his chest, kicking and squirming. I guess you don't get to where he's at without being tough.

It took a few days for the sheep to get used to their new home. Many of them were young, and this was their official weaning from mom. They bleated constantly, a sad, lost sound. I didn't think I could stand it much longer, but it finally stopped.

Part of my morning routine while feeding the back-field crew was to get a headcount on the sheep. The last thing I wanted was to lose one. One day, about a month in, I was short one. I headed for the back of the pasture, bracing myself for whatever I might find. Well, I *thought* I was braced. It turns out I wasn't.

Behind a big cedar tree near the back corner, I caught a flash of white through the branches. I walked around the edge, hoping there wasn't a coyote eating the sheep. There wasn't. Instead, there were *two* sheep, and one of them was only a few hours old. I pulled out my phone, took a picture and sent it to Erica.

Surprise! We're grandparents. Or grand foster parents, or something. Anyway, there's a new sheep.

We oohed and ahhed over it for a few minutes and took about a hundred pictures. The mom and the baby just stared at us like we were idiots. We probably deserved it. I couldn't believe how bright white the baby was. It practically glowed.

Over the next week, four more babies showed up. It got to the point that I couldn't remember how many sheep should be in the headcount each day, so I just started walking the pasture to make sure everyone was okay.

There is nothing cuter than babies. It doesn't matter if they're horses, donkeys, sheep, puppies, or whatever. Well, I will say that baby donkeys are probably cuter than anything else, but that doesn't take away from the incredible adorableness of baby sheep. They're just hilarious!

One morning, about a week after the sudden flurry of lamb arrivals, I noticed one of the babies was laying off by itself.

His mom was hanging out nearby, looking nervous. I wandered over to see what was going on.

Up to this point, you couldn't really get within fifteen feet of a sheep without it moving away. I knew something was wrong when the baby didn't stand up, and his mom stood her ground. I circled around, trying to grasp the situation.

The baby was sternal (that's a cool veterinary term I've learned. It means it's laying down, but its head is up and it's up on its chest, rather than down on its side) and it looked bright-eyed as it watched me walk around. I inched closer, but it still made no move to get up. As I got around the other side, I could see why. Its front right leg was pointing the wrong way, and not at a joint. It was obviously broken. I backed up and called Erica. Of course, she didn't have her phone on her. After all, we weren't on call, and we were feeding breakfast at seven am. The only reason I had my phone was to take sheep videos if one of them got the zoomies. (That's a term we coined for when a sheep starts bouncing around at nine hundred miles an hour.)

I took my shirt off and eased up to the baby, moving very slowly and talking to it the whole time. I didn't want it to run, and I also didn't want his mom to ram me. I squatted down and duck-walked the last few steps. Nobody moved, so that was good.

I laid my shirt on the ground next to the lamb. He bleated, and I stroked his side, trying to soothe him. That leg had to hurt like nobody's business, but he looked cheerful. He looked at me with his huge shining black eyes, and my heart broke. I assumed that we would have to euthanize him, as a broken leg is usually a death sentence for stock animals.

I eased my hands underneath his back, and carefully slid him onto my shirt. His broken leg was on top, so it didn't really move, to my relief. I tied the sleeves and tails of the shirt together, basically putting him inside a hobo sack. His mom stood stock still, watching me.

"I'm going to take your baby up to the barn," I said. "I don't know what's going to happen, but one way or the other, we're going to help him stop hurting." My eyes burned with tears and my nose was trying to run, and I couldn't even wipe it on my shirt sleeve. I hate moments like this.

I picked him up and started walking to the gate. His mom followed behind me, making me very nervous. If she rammed me, I would probably fall, and I didn't want to hurt the baby any more than he already was. When we got to the gate, she followed me out before I could stop her, and there was no getting her back in without setting the baby down. It looked like the three of us were going to the barn. Erica stood at the end of the aisle with her hands on her hips and a puzzled look on her face as we approached.

"Whatcha got going on there?"

"Baby sheep. His leg is broken. I couldn't get rid of his mom."

Always a veterinarian, Erica sprang into action. "Let me see."

She pulled back the edge of the shirt and peeked in for a second. The lamb bleated, and she stood up. "Put him in the empty stall. If his mom wants to go in, that's great. You might put some hay in there to keep her occupied. I gotta go grab my phone and do some calculations for dosing meds. Can you grab the scale out of mom's house and try to figure out how much he weighs?"

"I'm on it." I headed for the stall as Erica ran upstairs. The ewe followed me willingly enough, although she hesitated outside the stall door. I untied my shirt so the lamb could lay comfortably and went to grab a flake of alfalfa from the hay stall next door. As I guessed, the ewe was willing to follow the alfalfa into the stall. Looking back, that was probably the moment that she started caring about food more than she cared about her baby. I'm probably responsible for that, but it didn't occur to me in the moment that I was creating an alfalfa addict.

I ran across the driveway and grabbed the scale out of Erica's mom's bathroom. She was out of town, so that saved me about fifteen minutes of explaining what was going on. Erica was coming down the stairs as I returned.

"I don't have any of the right things for this," she said, as we headed into the stall. "Everything we carry is made for horses. I don't even have a syringe that makes measurements this tiny. And I haven't done conversions like this in a while, you may have to double check my math."

We carefully picked up the lamb with the shirt and set him on the scale. His head drooped off one side, and his feet dangled off the front. The needle on the scale didn't really move much.

"Okay, Plan B. I'll hold him and step on the scale, and you see what it says. Then we'll weigh me without him."

Erica nodded, and I picked the lamb up again. I hated to handle him so much, but getting the proper dose of pain killers was critical, especially as small as he was.

"208," Erica announced. I set him down gently and stepped back on the scale. "201."

"So, seven pounds," I said. "That seems awfully light. Does it sound right to you?"

She nodded. "He's about the same as the cats, maybe a few pounds lighter. He's only a week or two old, depending on which one he is."

We went out to the vet truck to gather what we needed. The medicines we carry are formulated for horses, so for something that would be a 2cc dose for a thousand-pound horse might only be 0.2 mls for the lamb. The math can get complicated, and there's no cheat sheet to make it easy. Erica read off the numbers, and we both did our own equation. Then she double checked another website to make sure the drug was safe for a nursing lamb. Once we were confident that we had the pain meds right, we did it again for the sedative we had to give him to set his leg bone back in place.

"I just thought of something," Erica said. "We've still got some insulin needles upstairs from the diabetic cat we fostered. Do you remember where they are?"

"On top of the fridge," I said. "I'll be right back." These syringes were much smaller than what we carry for horses, and the measurements were much more appropriate for what we needed. A moment later I returned with the needles. Erica drew up the medication, then we gathered the bandaging supplies and went back to the stall.

The next challenge for Erica was finding a vein. This is another way that horses spoil vets: their veins are huge! To her credit, she got it on the second try. As the needle went in, the lamb bleated pathetically. His mom raised her head and glanced over for a moment, alfalfa hanging out of her mouth, but then she went back to eating. Rather than pull the needle back out and stick a second one in for the second drug, Erica just pulled the syringe off the needle and stuck the second syringe on it. A moment later it was done, and we waited for the drugs to kick in.

"We need to splint this," Erica said. "Do we have a piece of PVC?"

I thought for a moment. "Yeah, I have a couple of small chunks. What size?"

Erica gave me a withering look. "I don't know, I'm not a plumber. Lamb leg size, with a wrap around it." She made a circle with her hands. "That big."

I went and scrounged in the garage and came back a minute later with a short piece of 2" PVC.

"Perfect! Now, we need to cut it in half, lengthwise."

I nodded. "I'll need your help with that. Do you want to do it now, or after you get him fixed up?" "Now. The sedation will take a bit to knock him out, but it won't last long, and I'd rather do this while he's out."

We measured the length of the pipe against his leg, then went back to the garage. I got a ruler and a Sharpie and drew a straight line down the side of the pipe, then handed it to Erica with a pair of gloves.

"I'm going to cut this with the SawzAll. I need you to hold it as tight as you can."

She grabbed it with both hands and braced it on the trash can where we store the horse feed. I lined up the blade and started cutting. As I got down to the middle, Erica moved her hands to the top. It was hard to keep it cutting straight, but I made it to the bottom without anyone getting hurt, so that was good. I smoothed out the edges with a piece of sandpaper, and we admired the finished product. The sides were wavy, and it was far from perfect.

"Well, it ain't pretty," I said.

"But it will work." Erica pointed to the door. "Come on, we're racing the clock."

When we got to the stall, the lamb was asleep. His mom was standing in the middle of the flake of alfalfa, with a smattering of green all over her. She didn't even look up when we walked in.

Erica put her stethoscope on and took a quick listen to his heart, and then we got to work. She injected a nerve-blocking drug in a few spots on his leg to further numb the pain, and then she gently manipulated the broken bone until it was back in position. I cringed, imagining how bad that had to hurt.

"Alright, I need you to hold his leg steady while I wrap it," she said. "Put your hands right here where mine are. Keep a bit of pressure on it so it doesn't slide apart, but don't push too hard."

"Ugh, no pressure, right?" I joked. "I'm in way over my head, here."

"Me, too," Erica said. "We don't get to do this with horses. If they break a leg, that's usually it, unless it goes to surgery. I haven't set a bone in years."

I gingerly held the leg. It was so small and fragile that I was terrified of hurting him worse. What if my hand twitched? What if I sneezed? I shook off the negative thoughts, lest I create my own bad luck.

Erica wrapped the leg with gauze to keep the tape from sticking to his leg hair, then covered it with an adhesive tape similar to an Ace bandage. It was strong, but still flexible. Next, she wrapped it with a thick cotton sheet.

"Okay, we'll put the splint on top of this. One piece in front, one piece in back. You hold it in place, I'll wrap."

"How come we're not putting a cast on it?" I asked.

"Well, for starters, I don't have casting material on the truck, that's at the clinic. But the main reason is that he's going to outgrow it every day or two. We'll have to rewrap this every other day, so it doesn't cut off circulation."

"Well, duh, that makes sense. I should have thought of that."

"Because you do this so much?" She grinned as she finished wrapping the splint. "Don't be so hard on yourself."

I had to laugh at myself. Erica is great about calling me out when I have unrealistic expectations of myself, and that has done wonders for my self-confidence. It's hard to be a perfectionist.

"Okay, now what?" I stood up and flexed my back.

"Now we wait for him to wake up and see how he does. We might have to help him stand up until he gets the hang of it."

"We need to call Ralph at some point," I said. "He needs to know one of his lambs got hurt. Speaking of which, I wonder how it happened? I haven't even had time to think about that."

Erica shook her head. "No telling. He might have gotten stepped on, or rammed, or just landed wrong. You know how they get to racing around, jumping over everything."

I knew. I might not admit it, but I had been spending more and more time out at the fence during the day, just watching them play. The older lambs were learning how to jump and buck and headbutt each other, and I found it endlessly amusing.

"Well, I'm sure it's happened at his house, too," I said.

Erica sighed. "Yeah, well, it's a commercial operation, don't forget that. It's not financially viable to do all this. They have to euthanize them if they get hurt too bad."

While the bookkeeper side of me totally understood that, the animal lover standing in front of the wounded lamb couldn't imagine it. "Do you think this guy will make it?" I asked.

"Oh yeah, he'll be good as new in a few months. They just need some time and support, especially at this age."

The lamb snorted, and we looked as he raised his head.

"Maaaaaa." His head flopped back down. The ewe glanced over at him and bleated back around a mouthful of hay. He was so cute that it was hard to look away from him.

"The mom really seems to like alfalfa," I said.

We gathered all our stuff and left the stall, closing the door behind us. I got a water bucket filled up for them and brought a couple bags of bedding in and spread it around. By the time the lamb was fully awake, I had the alfalfa in a hay net and everything else was put away. His mom was not impressed with the hay net.

It took him a few tries to stand up. He finally got there, and stood staring down at the bright yellow wrap on his leg for a minute. His ears flopped around, as he didn't have full muscle control yet. His head bobbed a few times, and then he hobbled over to his mom and started nursing with the leg stuck out sideways.

"Yeah," Erica said. "He's going to be fine." She headed off to work after a quick breakfast.

I tried to get some writing done, but I found myself checking the stall cameras every time I heard a sound downstairs in the barn. Sometimes he was sleeping, sometimes he was nursing, and sometimes he was in the blind corner where the camera couldn't see him. That was cause for several trips down to the stall. On the upside, I did get some great exercise going up and down the stairs to peek in on him. No matter what he was doing, awake or asleep, it was adorable.

That afternoon, three vet trucks rolled up in the driveway. I wasn't getting any work done anyway, so I went downstairs to see what was going on. The barn aisle was crowded with three vets, three techs, two vet students, and two very excited dogs. Erica caught my eye over the crowd.

"I showed them the pictures this morning, and everyone had to come see him."

I nodded. Who was I to throw stones? I'd been staring at him all day.

"What's his name?" Dr. Russel asked.

I shrugged. "We haven't named him yet."

There was a chorus of demands for a name. I don't know which one of them suggested it, but a minute later, his name was Gerald.

"He's totally a Gerald."

"That's hilarious! And he's so cute!"

I began to get a little jealous, which was weird. Gerald had been my obsession all day, and now everyone else was here, and he wasn't mine anymore. It's funny how people get possessive about ridiculous things, as if I wouldn't be able to appreciate all his cuteness if someone else was soaking it up. I did some quick self-counseling and got over it. Gerald was a great name, I had to admit.

Group visits like that became a regular thing. When it was time to change Gerald's leg wrap, everyone who wasn't busy came over to "help." Needless to say, he became comfortable with people really fast, and he became a bit of a Facebook celebrity. He also officially became our sheep. Ralph understood our attachment to him, and paying for all the vet care Gerald was getting was out of the question. So, Gerald became part of the family. I was tickled pink. Was there ever a time when I resisted the idea of having sheep? It was a distant memory, and I pretended like it never happened.

Gerald became very proficient at getting around on his splinted leg. At first, he took it slow, but as he became used to it and the pain went away, he got faster and faster. By the end of the first week, he had learned to use the splint as a pivot. When he got the zoomies, he would plant the splinted leg and run circles around it, like a race car drifting around a light pole. I was worried that all the activity would hinder the healing of his leg, but short of hanging him in a hammock, there wasn't much we could do to slow him down.

Cleaning the stall became one of my favorite parts of the day. Gerald loved to chase the shovel around. He was starting to headbutt everything, and I didn't want to teach him bad behavior, like headbutting people, because when he became a 150-pound sheep, that would really be a problem. So, I gave him a Pilates ball to push around. While I was shoveling poop, he would ram the ball, chasing it around the stall. I would kick the ball, and when it bounced off the wall, he would jump on it, riding it on his belly until it dumped him off the other side. As you can imagine, it could take an hour just to clean that one stall, but it was time well spent.

It was unbelievable how fast he grew. He learned to love alfalfa as much as his mom. We would stuff the hay net with Timothy hay and put a handful of alfalfa in the middle. They would then pull all the Timothy out of the hay net and eat the alfalfa, racing each other to get to it. Then they'd spend the rest of the day morosely munching on the Timothy. Like I said, we created a monster with the alfalfa. It took six weeks for his leg to heal enough to take the splint off, and by then he was nearly twice the size he was the day I carried him up to the barn.

Finally, the day came when Gerald and his mom (now named "Gerald's Mom") could go back out in the pasture with the other sheep. This was a big moment. Gerald had essentially spent his entire life in the barn. He had come in as a toddler and was leaving as a teenager. His voice was changing, cracking back and forth from a high octave to a low octave, which is by far one of the funniest sounds I've ever heard. I knew that sending him out to the pasture would mean much less time for us to spend together, but it would let him play with the other lambs and have some friends to grow up with.

I think being outside was scary for him at first. He had a lot of things to learn. For example, he'd been eating pelleted food and hay in addition to nursing, and had no idea what grazing was about. That was a major adjustment. He was also accustomed to sleeping in the security of the stall, and I think he felt vulnerable out in the wide-open pasture. He cried a lot for the first few days, which tore at my heartstrings.

Another unexpected side effect of having Gerald and Gerald's Mom living in a stall for six weeks was that they learned to associate people with food, and were quite tame. Gerald absolutely loved having his chest scratched, and while his mom wasn't fond of being touched, she was all about eating grain. This caused two things to happen.

First, when I went out to feed the horses and donkeys in the morning, Gerald and his mom would come running over, begging for food. The other sheep didn't know what to think about this, and it caused a lot of confusion for them. They are already disadvantaged in terms of their capacity for critical thinking, so now they were really in trouble. They could tell that Gerald's Mom knew something that they didn't know, and obviously whatever was in the bucket was amazing, but their instincts told them to run away from people. What ended up happening was that Gerald and his mom would rush the gate as I came in, fighting with the donkeys to get their head in the bucket. Five or six sheep would approach cautiously and stand a few feet away, watching. The rest of the sheep would run away, but they made a big deal about it, as it was splitting up the herd, and they weren't cool with that.

The other thing that happened was that it became almost impossible to herd the sheep from one pasture to another. Any time I went to push them towards the gate, Gerald, Gerald's Mom, and the other brave souls who converted to their way of thinking would run to me, while the others ran away. If you haven't tried pushing five sheep who are convinced you have food somewhere, let me tell you, it's like wading in hip-deep water with a strong current. You can't get much done.

We finally decided to put a couple of feed pans in the pasture and throw a handful of grain for the sheep every day. If we could get them all trained to food, then we could lead them from one pasture to another, rather than pushing them. We needed them to all be on the same page, and despite the fact that we hadn't fed Gerald or his mom any grain in a while, except what they were able to steal out of the bucket on occasion, they weren't giving up. So, we trained them to food. Guess what? This created a whole new set of things to happen. Who knew sheep would be so complicated?

Once all the sheep figured out the grain, I began getting mobbed in a whole new way. Most of them were still wild enough to keep their distance, but they grew bolder every day. I'm sure that Gerald was a bad influence on them, as he had no qualms about running up behind me and rearing up on his hind legs so he could jam his nose in the feed bucket. It was manageable when he was the only one doing it, but then there were three of them, sometimes four. The donkeys sensed the competition for the food.

Since the donkeys are fat and have way too much forage as it is, they only get a two-second nibble of food from the bucket.

This is mainly so we can catch them to give them vaccines and get their hooves trimmed. They've been getting the first bite every morning forever, and now there was a line of sheep trying to beat them to the bucket. At first they were able to bully the sheep out of the way, but Gerald quickly learned that they weren't going to actually eat him, and he started trying to jam his head in the feed bucket at the same time that Hannah Banana had her head in the bucket.

This ruckus caused delays in getting the horses their breakfast, and when I did make it over to the hay feeder where I dump their grain, the sheep were right there with me. Now I had to worry about the horses freaking out and kicking some sheep butt, and since there was food involved, it definitely could happen. Fortunately for everyone involved, the sheep figured out that some of the pellets fell through the cracks in the hay feeder and ended up on the ground underneath it. It was a slow evolution, but we finally got to the point where the sheep would crowd under the hay feeder, and only Gerald and his mom would fight for the bucket. It wasn't perfect, but it was a whole lot better than the sheep storm I'd been fighting.

One day Ralph came over with the trailer. It was time to load up some of the sheep and drop off some new ones. A lot of them were going to market, but some were going back to get bred. Gerald's Mom was on the list to go back to get bred. It was a forced weaning that he wasn't ready for, despite being too old to keep nursing. All of the incoming sheep were young ewes who had just been pulled from their mothers, so Gerald was not alone in his misery. Once again, we had to spend a few days listening to twenty crying sheep. I'm sure our neighbors were thrilled.

It took a few weeks for the new herd to come together. Since all the moms were gone, there was no seasoned leader.

Gerald became a co-leader of the group, probably because he knew his way around, and he appeared to be incredibly brave in his dealings with people. He was the only boy in the herd, and despite being neutered, I think he fancied himself a big ram. He quickly bonded with two young ewes. One had an ear tag that read *TWEAK* and the other was 908. The three have become inseparable. Gerald has taught them how to eat grain out of the bucket in the mornings, and how to mill around the horses and donkeys without getting kicked or stepped on.

We've taken to giving the sheep the run of the place. They get locked in their pasture at night so the donkeys can protect them, but during the day, we leave enough slack in the gate chain that the sheep can get in and out. They've done a terrific job of weeding the place. They've even cleaned up the woods, or at least the bottom three feet. The only downside of building a mostly tame herd of sheep is that they're brave enough to walk into the barn, and apparently, they like pooping on concrete. Gerald has also learned that if Erica is working with one of the horses, she probably has treats in her pocket. He has no problem walking up and demanding a bite while she's jumping Ernie around in the arena or doing groundwork with Vespa. He just walks right up and bats his eyelashes. Of course, it gets him what he wants. How can you say no to that face?

Chapter 6

ERNIE'S ENTRAPMENT

ERICA'S FAVORITE HORSE IS AN OFF THE TRACK Thoroughbred named Ernie. She does show jumping, and Ernie is her
star. I have my challenges with Ernie, and he has his challenges
with me. Part of the problem is that he's Erica's number one,
and has been since before I met her. Then I came in, and
I'm also Erica's number one, and neither of us like sharing her.
Erica says we don't get along because we're very much
alike. Not in that we're both ridiculously good looking and
charming, just to be clear (I checked). It's more that we're both
high-strung, sensitive, emotional over-achievers. Having had
several years of therapy, I know that's code for 'emotionally
challenged.' I've made a lot of progress (and so has Ernie, if I'm

being honest), but Ernie shows me where I'm still lacking.

Just for the record, I get along with all the other horses just fine, as well as both donkeys, both dogs, the sheep, and all the cats except for one. I'm very much an animal guy. It's just a personality conflict with Ernie, and most of the time we do our job and ignore each other. We're not at war, or anything like that.

One Tuesday evening, I was headed home from the clinic, driving along behind Erica. Without warning, she shot ahead down the road, leaving me behind. A moment later my phone rang. It was Erica.

"Hey."

"Bridget just called. Ernie's colicking bad, throwing himself on the ground." Bridget was the college student that we hired to take care of the barn in the evenings. She knows horses, and she's not prone to panic. If she said it was bad, I believed her. Based on Erica's vet truck dwindling to a speck in the distance, she did, too. I put my foot down, and my old pickup slowly gained speed.

"I'm right behind you," I said. "I'll be right there."

"Alright. I love you."

"Drive careful."

As a numbers nerd, I do all kinds of math problems, just for fun. For example, our vet clinic is located next to a lime rock quarry. That means we have dump trucks going up and down our road all the time. Sometimes they get reckless and try to pass each other, or other cars, on the 2-lane road. While I understand that they get paid by the load, I had to do the math to see if driving faster would actually help them make more money.

I took the distance between the lime rock quarry and the red light in the next town and did some calculations. Assuming there was no other traffic causing delays, such as a turning car or a school bus, the most time you could possibly save by going

70 in a 55 zone is about a minute and a half. In reality, there's always traffic turning, so you couldn't shave more than one minute off your time by speeding the whole ten miles. That means no matter how fast they go, or how slow, they're going to get the same number of trips in per day. I emailed that breakdown to the safety officer of the dump truck company, but I never heard back from him. On the upside, the dump trucks don't pass each other much these days, so maybe he explained it to them after all.

Our house is only about a five-mile drive from the clinic, and we were already halfway home, but I didn't bother telling Erica that she was only going to get there about fifteen seconds sooner by speeding. In an emergency, you have to do something to feel like you're responding appropriately, whether it's actually helping or not. That's just part of being human. I can't throw stones. I was speeding now, too, even though I knew it was pointless. Such is life.

Ernie was laying in his stall when we arrived. Bridget gave us the rundown on what she knew as Erica got a halter on him and prodded him to stand up.

"He was fine when I was dumping feed," Bridget said. "I went out back to feed the donkeys, and when I got back, he was thrashing around like crazy. I don't what could have happened so fast. He didn't even eat."

My mind immediately went to a twist, as most horse people's minds probably do. Having been to a lot of colic emergencies with Erica and listened to her explain to people how a twist works, I knew it was entirely possible, and that it happens in an instant. Twists occur when the gut is trying to move something through and ends up spasming. Because it's only attached to the abdomen in one place, if the large colon contracts hard enough, it can flip itself over, creating a kink. This is excruciatingly painful for horses, and they react by throwing themselves on the ground, rolling around, and trying to ease the abdominal pain. A lot of people think the twist happens from the rolling, but it's the other way around. Erica once responded to a twist that occurred while the horse was standing on the crossties after being ridden. It hadn't rolled in hours, if not longer.

Once Erica had a halter on Ernie, I held his head while she checked his heart rate and got some sedation and pain meds into him. There was no way she could palpate him to see what was going on until he was calmed down. If he threw himself down while she had her arm inside him, that could be the end of the world. I watched carefully as she worked, ready to do whatever she needed. This was as stressful as it can get for Erica.

"What's his heart rate?" I asked, trying to get her talking.

"Sixty." That was high, but not through the roof. She drew a bit of blood in a syringe and handed it to me. "Can you run a lactate quick? The meter's on the window sill."

A lactate test is exactly like a blood sugar test for a diabetic. I stuck a test strip in the meter and squirted a drop of blood onto the end of it. It takes thirteen seconds to give you a result, which probably felt like an hour for Erica. I relaxed when it finally gave me the number.

"2.3." Anything under three is considered normal for a horse. If it goes higher, that's a strong indicator that all is not well inside. For example, if a lipoma gets wrapped around the small intestine and cuts off circulation, the lactate will often jump to five or six.

Erica nodded curtly and pulled a palpation sleeve on. I grabbed Ernie's lead rope. His head was starting to droop, and his breathing had slowed down some. She squirted lube on her hand and arm and pulled his tail aside.

I've never palpated a horse, of course, but I can't imagine how scary it would be to stick my arm inside their butt and keep going until I'm in up to my shoulder, especially when they're sick and might drop to the ground without warning. So many things can go wrong. I think about every single one of those things when I'm holding a horse for Erica to palpate. What if the horse jerks to one side? What if it kicks her? What if he falls? What would I do? So many things to stress about.

I couldn't tell what she felt from the look on her face. It was a mask of concentration, and I knew better than to ask while she was working on him. To Ernie's credit, he stood still the whole time. I rubbed between his ears and told him a bunch of things I didn't really believe, such as, *You're a good boy*, and things like that. When it's crunch time, you gotta play the game.

"Can you grab the ultrasound?" she asked, pulling her arm out. "I don't feel anything abnormal, definitely nothing to explain why he's so painful."

I draped the lead rope across Ernie's neck and jogged around the corner to the vet truck. Like the digital x-ray, the ultrasound lives in a big suitcase and weighs a ton. The advantage to the ultrasound machine is that the case has wheels, and our barn has a concrete aisleway, so I was able to roll it most of the way.

I had unpacked the ultrasound and was attaching the probe when Ernie started looking at his side. He blew out a hard breath and flexed his knees. I knew that meant he was trying to lay down, and that wasn't good. I set the ultrasound on the bench and grabbed his lead rope to try and keep him on his feet. Erica was already pulling up another syringe of sedation.

"That didn't last long," I said. "Do you think he's immune to the drugs?"

She slid the needle into the vein on his neck. "No, it means he's in serious pain." Her face was drawn and pale. I felt helpless, which is not an emotion I handle well. If something is wrong in Erica's world, I like to find solutions. With Ernie, there was nothing I could do except support her in whatever way she needed. Right now, she needed me to be a good tech, so I resolved to do the best I could and be content with my contribution.

It took a minute, but Ernie calmed back down. I grabbed the ultrasound and held it as she soaked his abdomen with alcohol and began scanning his gut. It was hard to be quiet, but she needed to focus, and she wasn't in a good place for a million questions. I shifted my thoughts to what all might happen next. It was quite possible that Ernie would be going to Ocala for surgery. Was the truck full of fuel? I tried to remember the last time I parked it. We had gone to Ocala to Erica's trainer on Saturday, and the truck and trailer were still connected. I was pretty sure it had at least a half a tank of diesel.

Erica guided us around to the other side of the horse. Ernie stood still, his head hanging down to his knees. The intensity of Erica's gaze as she stared at the screen was a bit scary, especially when she found the abnormality.

"He's got some distended small intestine." She pushed some buttons on the machine. "Some of these loops have a thickened wall."

"What does that mean?"

"It means something bad is going on in there, and we're going to EMC." EMC is the referral hospital in Ocala where we send our surgical cases.

"Right now?"

"Right now."

I left her to pack up the ultrasound and went to get the truck and trailer pulled around. By the time I got the ramp dropped, she was standing there with Ernie. He loaded willingly enough, and Erica gave him a bit more pain medicine for the drive. He'd be on the trailer for forty-five minutes, and we didn't want him thrashing around and hurting himself even more. As soon as we got in the truck, Erica called ahead to let them know we were coming. It was nearly 7:45 pm when we got there.

I've hauled a variety of horses to EMC before, but never one of our own. Up to this point, my involvement usually ended when the techs walked the horse off the trailer, and I returned home. Tonight was different. Not only was I staying, I got to watch everything. Perks of being a horse doctor's husband.

I'm always looking for ways to help other horse people learn more about horse things, and I realized right away that this was an incredible opportunity for that. With the permission of the surgeon, I pulled out my phone and started recording the process. They started by putting Ernie in the stocks and doing the same workup that Erica had done initially. While that was going on, an intern talked to Erica about all the drugs she'd given Ernie, what his vitals were on the initial workup, and all those details.

"Is he a cribber?" the surgeon asked when they were finished.

Erica nodded. "Yep. Are you thinking entrapment?"

"Well, that's the most probable. His small intestine definitely isn't happy, and the way he's blowing through sedation, he's really painful. I don't find anything abnormal on palpation.

I think we definitely need to put him on the table and open him up. We might find something else, but I think it'll be an epiploic foramen entrapment."

Erica nodded. "Alright, let's do it."

The team sprang into action, and it was hard to keep up with what was going on. The intern shaved a square place on Ernie's neck, placed a catheter, and sutured it in place while the surgeon and his team went to scrub and suit up.

"What do we do?" I asked Erica. She was walking rapidly down the hall, and I was nearly jogging to keep up. That's kind of funny, considering that I'm nearly a foot taller than her.

"We scrub and suit up," she said, as if it were obvious. "I'm not going to sit out here while they do surgery. Are you?"

"Are we allowed to go in there?"

"Since I'm a vet, yes. You get in as my plus one."

"Then I'm going in, too. I didn't know that was an option."

My mind was in high gear as I imagined what it would be like. I'd never been in a surgery suite before, and I had no idea what to expect. Erica directed me through a door which led to a locker room.

"There's clean scrubs in those bins. You need top and bottoms. Put your clothes in a locker, put on a scrub hat from that stack there, and use those Crocs by the door. I'll meet you inside."

My eyebrows shot up. "Crocs? I'm wearing someone else's sandals?"

"They've been sterilized, dear. Everything is clean. You can't take in outside stuff."

That made sense. She disappeared around the corner on the women's side, and I set about suiting up. Having never done any of this before, I felt silly when I walked through the door into the prep room, even though I looked exactly like everyone else. I'm tall and skinny, and my pants were made for someone short and fat. They were baggy in the crotch and six inches short in the ankle, and the crocks were too big. The scrub top fit okay, but they have a different fit than a normal shirt, and I felt weird. I hid my discomfort behind the paper mask and looked around.

The prep room was huge, and nothing like what I thought it would be. It was very industrial and utilitarian. The concrete floor was painted gray, and the concrete block walls were painted white with various hose fittings and connections sticking out here and there. The white ceiling was high and featured an overhead crane on an I-beam. I followed the rest of the crew to a door at the far end.

Someone in front of me opened the door, and the first thing I noticed was that the door was a foot thick. Upon closer inspection, the door itself wasn't that thick, but it had a thick green pad attached to it. The rest of the room was the same, with padded walls, a padded floor, and a padded door on the opposite wall leading out to the exam area where Ernie had been the last time I saw him.

Ernie was standing against the left wall in the padded room with a technician holding his halter and scratching his neck. Once the rest of the team was ready, they swung out a section of the rear wall, creating a padded stall around him. The intern gave him a shot, and a moment later he crumpled to the floor. As soon as he was down, the room became a hive of activity.

"Back up," Erica said, grabbing my arm.

I was trying to film everything and take photos of the process, but since I didn't know what they were doing, I ended up being in the way. I was glad Erica was there to steer me around.

As soon as I stepped to the side, someone came past me with a handful of big yellow straps. Having worked in a few different industries in my life, I recognized them as being nylon sling straps, like you would use to pick things up with a crane. A light bulb popped on in my head, and suddenly it all started making sense.

"I get it," I whispered to Erica. "They're going to pick Ernie up with the crane, right?"

"Right. It's really hard to get a horse to lay down on a table. There's only so many ways you can get that done."

With the folding wall stowed away, they rolled Ernie over and secured the straps to his legs while the intern inserted a tube into his mouth. Another anonymous person in scrubs and a mask grabbed the crane control and dropped the hook down to his belly. A moment later, they hoisted him up until his head cleared the floor, and the crane slowly moved him towards us and out the door.

We moved out of the way again, and someone else rolled a surgery table under Ernie. It looked like a gurney, except that it was bigger and really heavy duty. They spent a lot of time getting him positioned just right. He was on his back with all four legs pointing up. Pipes slid vertically into mounts on the sides of the table, with big pads on them to keep him from rolling sideways. His head was similarly supported so that it stayed in position.

"They're pretty fussy about this," I whispered to Erica.

"Horses aren't designed to lay on their back," she whispered back. "Everything needs to be just right to minimize the risk of secondary problems."

As soon as they had him where they wanted him on the

table, the intern who had inserted the tube in his mouth rolled an IV tree over and started hanging bags of fluids. Some were large, and some were small, but they all fed to a single tube which she attached to the catheter in Ernie's neck.

The surgery team was busy doing other things as well. Ernie's feet got wrapped and strapped to the table so he wouldn't kick anyone if he twitched, his belly got shaved, and he got scrubbed cleaner than he's ever been in his life. It was incredible how dirty he was, despite getting washed on a regular basis. Their clipping system was very impressive. A shop vac hose attached right into the wall, and while one person clipped him, another sucked the hair up. I leaned over to Erica.

"We need a setup like that at home."

"We're not doing colic surgery at home."

"No, the vacuum," I said. "For when you clip the horses. This is way better than trying to sweep hair off the mats." She nodded, but I could tell she was still stressed out. I decided to leave it alone. This was all new and exciting for me, but it was neither for her.

Once his belly was clipped and clean, everyone gathered around the table and began pushing. I hadn't even noticed the double doors when I came into the prep room. The anesthesia team backed through the doors first, rolling the IV tree and holding the tubes going to Ernie's neck so that everything stayed in place. I came in last and filmed them as they positioned the table under a giant light in the operating room.

As soon as they locked the wheels, the anesthesia team hooked a hose to the tube in Ernie's mouth and placed some sensors on him. His heartbeat pulsed across a monitor a moment later, complete with the expected beep, and I almost giggled with delight. This was just like something from a movie!

I was so enthralled with the tech gadgets that I had to remind myself how serious this was, and that there were no guarantees on the outcome. I kept my mouth shut and continued recording. I already knew we were going to be able to make a great video on colic surgery for our YouTube channel.

Ernie got scrubbed again and covered in blue sheets. Soon the only part of him that was visible was his head and a square on his belly. I stopped recording for a bit to give my arms a break and walked over beside Erica.

"Who are all these people?" I asked. "Do you know the roles?"

"Yep. You know the surgeon, he's in charge. He has an intern who will do the surgery with him, and he's teaching her. There's another intern running anesthesia, and she's got an extern shadowing her. Then you've got the surgery nurse, a technician, and two more externs."

"The externs are vet students here on like a two-week rotation, right?"

"Right. They're all third- and fourth-year vet students. They'll be hoping to get an internship here when they graduate."

"How long is an internship?"

"One year."

"And then they go on to work at a practice somewhere?"

"Sometimes. They might start their own practice or get a job at a referral hospital like this, or even at a vet school. There're lots of options."

I shook my head. Every time I start thinking I've figured out how it all works, another layer is exposed, and I realize it's all way more complicated than I thought. At this point, I've learned that kids start volunteering at veterinary clinics and animal shelters in high school to start gaining experience, and they're 27-30 years old before they become a full-time doctor on their own. I'm very impressed with that kind of tenacity and clarity of direction, because when I was in high school... well, that's another story. Let's just say that when I was 35, I still didn't know what I wanted to be when I grew up. The focus and support that these kids have makes me realize how diverse the world really is. My experience wasn't like that at all.

Erica nudged me with her elbow. "They're starting."

I got my phone out and found a good spot near Ernie's head where I was out of the way and still had a decent view. The surgeon was running his finger down Ernie's stomach and talking to the intern across from him. It was difficult to understand what they were saying with the masks on. A moment later, a scalpel appeared in his hand, and he made a slice right down Ernie's belly. They pulled his cecum out of the incision, and I was surprised at how little blood there was. It was filled with gas, and the surgeon examined it for a moment, then called over to Erica.

"Has he had colic surgery before?"

Erica shook her head. "No, not that I know of. Why?"

The surgeon beckoned her over. "I think he has. Check this out. It looks like some of it's missing, and there's some scar tissue here."

"Huh. I got him when he was three, so it's possible he went before then." They shared a knowing glance.

"I guess they forgot to mention that part when you bought him."

"Yeah. They didn't mention his retroverting epiglottis or his collapsing pharynx, either. It's a good thing he's so charming and scopey."

I've never purchased a horse, but it seems like those are some pretty big things to not mention to someone who's paying thousands of dollars for an athlete. There are some shady people in this world.

Erica stepped back and the surgeon reached inside Ernie's belly and felt around. I could tell from his gestures with his free hand that he was explaining something to the intern, but I couldn't hear them. A moment later he pulled his arm out, and she put her arm in. He guided her from the outside, pointing to different areas. She nodded. Her arm was buried up to the shoulder inside his abdomen.

They traded places again, and the surgeon's arm disappeared up to the shoulder. "Epiploic foramen," he called out.

"What does that mean?" I whispered to Erica.

"It means he has an epiploic foramen entrapment," she said. "There's a place where the liver, stomach and pancreas come together, and it creates a hole, or a space between them. Sometimes, mainly in horses that are cribbers, the small intestine goes through that hole and gets stuck. It happens in people, too."

"So, that's what's so painful?"

"Basically. Once it goes through there, the intestine spasms, and then it's being squeezed, and that hurts, so it spasms, and more and more of it gets forced through the hole. It's a vicious cycle."

I shuddered at the thought. "What do they do about it? Just pull it back out?"

"Yep. The small intestine is delicate, so it tears easy. They have to be super careful pulling it out. Depending on how much has gone through, this might take a while. See how far inside it is?"

I nodded.

"They're feeding it out a tiny bit at a time with their fingertips. I had to do a couple of these in my internship, and they're exhausting. I'm getting a hand cramp just thinking about it."

"Me, too," I said. "At least they can take turns with it."

It ended up taking over two hours. I didn't record much of that part, as all the action was taking place inside of Ernie. From outward appearances, they were just standing there leaning over Ernie at awkward angles. It's interesting how physically intense something like that can be. I never would have thought about that aspect of surgery, but it's brutal on the doctor's back.

By midnight, I was dead on my feet. I had long since lost all my enthusiasm for the experience. A stereo was playing dance music, and that was the only thing that kept me even remotely awake. I'm one of those people that crashes at nine pm sharp, like someone turns my switch off. A sudden flurry of activity brought me out of my stupor.

At the surgery table, the surgeon and the intern were pulling mountains of Ernie's intestines out and stacking them carefully around the incision area on the sterile sheet.

"What are they doing?" I asked.

"They got everything out, and now they have to inspect it to make sure none of it got compromised."

"How do you know if it got compromised?"

"The color," Erica said. "See how it's all pink? They're looking for dark spots, like purple splotches. That's a compromised bowel."

"What happens if they find one of those?"

"They have to cut it out. We're hoping that doesn't happen."

I lapsed into silence, watching the process intently and searching for any discoloration. It was hard to believe that all those guts had come out of Ernie's belly, and even harder to believe they were all going back in. I don't even like trying to jam excessive clothes in a suitcase, and you can be rough with those. This looked like an unfixable mess to me. There was nothing wrong with Ernie's intestines, and somehow it all went back inside. Part of me knew that it would, since that's what these people do every day, but I still didn't see how it could. I remembered to film some of it as they were finishing up, and a few minutes later they were sewing his belly shut. Erica walked over, and I trailed behind her.

"Well, his intestine looked good," she said.

"Yeah, I like everything," the surgeon replied. "His color was good, no tears anywhere, all good stuff. I feel pretty good about it. If we can get his incision healed up without an infection, I'd say he'll be fine."

I glanced at Erica. "Is that a common problem?"

"Yep. Most owners worry about the horse surviving surgery. We worry about them surviving the recovery. That's where most of the danger is."

They removed the sterile sheets, which were now a bloody mess, and disconnected the anesthesia. When everyone was ready, they wheeled him back out to the prep room, lifted him off the table with the crane, and put him in another padded room.

"This is the worst part for me," Erica said. We stood in the hallway and peered through a tiny window at Ernie's sleeping hulk on the floor inside the green room.

"Waiting for him to wake up?"

"Not that, so much, but getting him back on his feet. He'll want to stand up as soon as he wakes up, but he'll still be groggy. It's the most dangerous part of the whole thing, because they can easily break a leg."

"Ahh, I see." I grabbed her hand and squeezed it. I thought of a thousand things to say, but nothing would comfort her until he stood up safely, so I just held her hand.

It took forever, but Ernie finally woke up. They gave him another shot to keep him calm while he got himself together. It was 2:00 am when he finally got to his feet. The stress melted from Erica's face as she pressed her forehead against the window, and I rubbed her neck and shoulders as she watched him sway. It had been an incredibly long night, but we were finally out of the woods, at least for now.

I don't remember the drive home, but somehow, we made it. We had time for a shower and about three hours of sleep before we had to get up and go to work. I was a zombie.

Ernie got to come home after a few days and recover in his own stall. This doesn't normally get to happen, but since Erica is a veterinarian, she got special treatment. He was on stall rest for a long time, which he was not happy about at all. There were lots of bandage changes, medications, hours of hand-walking and grazing, and that sort of thing. He did develop an infection in his incision after a few weeks, but we caught it right away and managed it. Three months later, he was given the all clear to go back out in the pasture at night and start getting back in shape.

I learned an awful lot during this experience, and I wanted to share some of the important things with you. If you have a horse, you might find these things helpful.

- **Have a plan.** You need to decide *now* whether or not each horse you have will go to surgery if it ever becomes necessary. Colic surgery is expensive. The alternative is euthanasia. You don't want to have to reason that out and come to a decision in the heat of the moment when your horse is throwing himself on the ground and the vet needs to know what you want to do.

- **Money.** If surgery is an option for you, put some money aside in an emergency account. Even if you can only put $50 a month in there, it will build up over time. If the emergency happens, you'll be better prepared to pay for it. If it never happens, you can splurge on something else someday.

- **Have a transportation plan.** Many people who have horses do not have a trailer to haul them. If you are one of these people, you need to make arrangements now with someone who does have a trailer to haul your horse in an emergency. This is not something to deal with at midnight, when your horse needs surgery immediately. If you can't find someone you know, find a professional service that's available 24/7 and put their number in your phone.

- **Do all the stuff they tell you to do in recovery.** The medicine regimen, the wound care and cleaning, the bandage changes, the vet visits, everything. Is it going to be expensive? Yes. Is it going to be time consuming? Yes. Will your horse suffer if you don't? Yes. If you're willing to put your horse through surgery, be willing to go the extra mile afterwards. The worst tragedy is when a horse makes it through all the hard stuff and then dies from an infection because someone was slacking on aftercare.

Okay, back to Ernie. He lost about three hundred pounds during his ordeal, and it took a while to get him back up to weight. He's a Thoroughbred, so it's hard to keep weight on him, anyway. Erica spent hours doing groundwork with him to get his muscles built back up. She was ecstatic when she was able to start riding him again. A little over a year from his surgery, he went to his first post-recovery horse show. It was an exciting milestone, even for me.

Ernie and I still aren't best friends, but something about that whole experience changed my perspective on our relationship. I don't know if it was seeing his guts laid out on the surgery table, or the hundreds of hours I spent hand-grazing him in the months following his surgery, or realizing just how important he is to Erica. Maybe it was all those things. Whatever it was, I'm a bit more tolerant of him now. Sometimes I even mean it when I tell him things like, *Good boy*. Not always, but sometimes. It's progress.

Chapter 7

A Load of Sand

I am truly blessed in so many ways. One of those ways is that I'm a morning person. I have no problem falling asleep at night, and my eyes pop open somewhere between 4:00 am and 5:00 am every morning. I know, this probably sounds terrible to you, but I haven't had to wake up to an alarm in years, and that is a wonderful thing. By extension of this, Erica hasn't had to wake up to an alarm much, either, as I wake her up. Not at 4:00 am, mind you. More like 6:00 am.

The downside to this is that on the rare occasion that we do set an alarm for something, I struggle to identify the sound, and I wake up confused. Part of that is probably due to changes in technology. Back in my younger days, when I did use an alarm clock, it was a real alarm clock, the kind that sounds like a fire alarm incessantly buzzing. Now we use our phones for this, and the sound is completely different.

On this particular night, I woke up in that state of confusion over and over. We had a colic horse in the clinic, and Erica was worried about him. She set an alarm on her phone to go off every hour, all night long, so that she could check on him. Technology has made this process a lot better than it used to be. Instead of driving to the clinic every hour, or staying there all night like we used to do, we have cameras in the stalls now, which we can check from our phones. All she really needed to see was that he was standing quietly, and not rolling.

I slept through the first alarm, which I determined when I woke up at 11:00 pm, wondering what in the world that noise could be. Erica grabbed her phone and silenced the alarm, and I realized what was going on. I went back to sleep.

The second time I woke up, I still had no idea what the sound was, as my brain had incorporated it into my dream. I was driving, and every radio station was playing the same strange song. When I opened my eyes, Erica was holding her phone, which was playing the same song as the radio in my dream, and I couldn't figure out how that was possible.

"What are you doing?" I asked, glancing at the clock on my nightstand. It was midnight.

"Checking on the horse." She opened the camera app on her phone, and it all started coming back to me.

At 1:00 am, I growled into my pillow. This time I knew exactly what the sound was, and I would have sworn that I had just heard it two minutes before. Sleeping an hour at a time is brutal.

"He's down," Erica said. I jammed my head under the

pillow, but she didn't go away. "He's looking at his side again. We need to go to the clinic."

At that moment, I didn't think that I had ever been more tired in my life. The last thing I wanted to do was get out of bed. "I don't wanna go to school," I mumbled.

Erica turned on her bedside lamp and sat up. She's way better at the nighttime stuff than I am. "Are you coming with me?"

Guilt is a great motivator for me. All she has to do is suggest that I stay at home in bed while she goes to work, and I'm up. If I did stay home, all I would do is lay in bed and feel like a schmuck. I pulled my head out from under the pillow. "Yeah, yeah, I'm coming."

Bleary-eyed and zombie-like, I swallowed a glass of water and staggered down to the truck. The drive to the clinic was quiet. Erica watched the horse on her phone, and I watched the eyeballs in the ditch, willing them to stay there. Fortunately for everyone involved, no wildlife made bad decisions during the ten-minute trip.

The horse was lying down when we arrived. The four bags of IV fluids hanging from the ceiling were still a quarter full, and the curly-q tube between the bags and the horse reminded me of an old phone cord, only bigger. I was probably delirious from lack of sleep, but I had a crazy urge to wrap it around my finger like I did when I was a kid.

"What's wrong with him?" I asked. "Gas colic?"

Erica shook her head as she prodded him to stand up. "Sand colic. He's got a ton of sand in his gut."

"I didn't know you brought them in for that," I said. The horse stood up. "Don't we usually just give them the powder stuff and call it a day?"

"Can you grab the lube?" She was pulling on a palpation sleeve, and I handed her the tube from the windowsill. "Most of the time that's all they need. This one's a little different. He's not passing it very well, so we're giving him a major flush. And it's psyllium, by the way. Psyllium, Epsom salt, and a lot of water. Zulu even got some mineral oil yesterday."

I held the lead rope as she palpated the horse, but he wasn't trying to go anywhere. Erica felt around for a minute, then pulled her arm back out. She pulled the glove off, turning it inside out around her hand. There was a small handful of poop on the inside.

"Let's put some water in this," she said, stepping outside the stall. I followed her over to the sink and cracked the faucet. "Right there, stop. Perfect."

She tied the glove off and shook it lightly a few times, then held it up to the light. We watched as it settled out. The water turned yellowish green with particles floating around the top, and the fingers began to fill up with sand. It was impressive to see just how much sand was in that small bit of poop.

"Yesterday, there was hardly any sand," she said.

My eyebrows shot up. "Does that mean he's getting it here? Are we exposing him to more sand somehow?"

"No, silly," Erica said with a laugh. "That means he wasn't moving it out of his gut before, and now he is."

I was a little embarrassed that I didn't think of that, but since it was the middle of the night, I went easy on myself. "Oh. Well, that makes sense. How come he wasn't passing it? It just rests on the bottom of the intestines, right?"

"Sort of." She drew a string of w's in the air with her finger. "The large colon is ridged so it can expand with gas and stuff coming through it. The sand sits in those low spots, and sometimes the food moving through there stops being able to pick it up. That's what's going on with Zulu."

A lightbulb was going on in my head. I might think slower at 2:00 am, but I get there eventually. "So, the Epsom salt and the powder stuff can grab it as it goes through."

"Right."

Suddenly there was a massive fart sound from the stall beside us, followed by the unmistakable sound of projectile diarrhea. My eyes widened as I stared at Erica. "Was that the sound of success? Because it sounded messy."

She stepped past me and walked over to Zulu's window. "That's the unavoidable downside of flushing them like this. They get the runs like you wouldn't believe. That's why we have to keep them on fluids, or else they'll dehydrate and colic all over again. On the upside, there's probably a ton of sand in that."

I moved over beside her and gazed at the mess of watery poop splatters running down the stall wall. "It looks like the pressure washer is going to earn its keep."

Erica chuckled. "Yeah, you can't do much about the mess. That's why his tail is wrapped."

I hadn't noticed before, but Zulu's tail was braided and encased in VetRap like a sausage dog. It was a nice touch.

"I guess that's why he was down, then, huh?" I asked. "He was probably cramping with all that coming down the line."

Erica nodded. "Probably."

"You're lucky that didn't happen while you were palpating him. That would have been bad." We both laughed at the thought. "I would've felt bad spraying you down with the water hose, but you couldn't ride home like that."

"Nah, that's why we have a shower and a washing machine here," she said. "You think that's never happened before?"

I pursed my lips. "I guess it never occurred to me." Once again, I had a glimpse into the side of veterinary medicine that I don't see very often. Working from home is wonderful, but I miss out on things like that. Not that it's something I want to see, of course.

"Bob Stafford had to take a shower and do laundry here just a few weeks ago," she said.

"Bob the farrier?"

"Yep. He was working on a horse right here in the aisle. He had her left rear foot up on his thigh, tacking the shoe on, and she just started peeing. It soaked his whole shoulder and left side."

"Oh, my God, that must have been horrible!" I laughed, trying to picture the moment. It had to be a terrible sensation; hot urine running down your side, stinking and saturating everything. I gave myself the heebie-jeebies imagining it.

"Oh, it was bad," she agreed. "He had to finish putting that shoe on before he could do anything, since he already had a nail in it. For him, though, I think it was even worse having to sit in the clinic in the spare scrub top and pants for an hour and a half while his clothes went through the laundry. You know how big he is, and the scrubs are smalls. He looked hilarious, and being in an office full of girls was probably hard on his ego."

Zulu let out another jet of steaming diarrhea, punctuated with loud farts and a few groans. I knew it wasn't pleasant for him, but it had to be better than the cramping and the weight of a gut full of sand.

"I should see if I can find the footage of that on the security cameras," I said with a grin. "That would be great blackmail material!"

"Which part?" Erica asked. "Him getting peed on, or him

in a half shirt with pants that didn't quite go up as high as they should?"

It was funny, but I felt a little bad for Bob. He was a good guy. I doubted that it was the first time a horse had put him in a bad spot, though. Animals have a way of keeping our feet on the ground. The beauty of it is that you can't even accuse them of being malicious or trying to teach us a lesson out of some sense of superiority. It's just the universe reminding us that there are more important things in life than our image. Like the need to pee.

We hung out with Zulu a bit longer, but now that he was passing everything, it was pretty much just a matter of riding it out and keeping him hydrated. We hung another bag of fluids before we left, and Erica cleaned up the worst of the mess in case he decided to lay down again. It was a small thing, but affording him that dignity is one of the things that makes me admire her so much.

When we got home, I was asleep within minutes of hitting the bed. I don't know if Erica's alarm went off after that, or not. If it did, I slept through it. When my eyes popped open, I was horrified to see that the sun was up, and it was nearly 7:00 am. I had really slept in. In the back field, the donkeys began braying, announcing that another day had begun, and it was time for breakfast. That's farm life. No matter what happened the night before, you still have to maintain the routine. If you're a minute late, you'll hear about it!

Chapter 8

SERIOUSLY, THOSE DONKEYS

OUT OF ALL THE ANIMALS THAT WE HAVE, which is a lot, there is just something about the donkeys that I love. Perhaps it's the way they appreciate getting their back scratched, or their winter coat brushed off. Perhaps it's the fun of watching them run around when they get excited. Or, maybe it's their independent spirit and determination to not be coerced into anything they don't want to do. I don't know what it is, really, but the donkeys are my people.

They like to test my commitment to the friendship sometimes. You know, just to make sure I really mean it. One of their favorite times to put me to the test is when I'm bringing them a new bale of hay.

We have these big wooden tables under the shades out in the pastures where we put the hay. They're about waist high, or maybe a bit more. The hay goes in a net on the table, and the net gets tied to the rafters. It's a good system, and we use it with the 500-pound blocks of alfalfa as well as round rolls. The hay is up off the ground so the sheep can't get to it and the horses can't get a hoof or shoe stuck in the net. The nets are slow-feed nets, so they have small holes that keep the horses and donkeys from eating too fast. Finally, there's almost no wasted hay, because it's up on the table and everything gets eaten.

For the front fields, putting a new bale out isn't a big deal. The horses are in the barn during the day, so it's just a matter of driving out in the pasture, backing up to the table, and unloading. For the back field, where the donkeys live, it's a whole different experience.

Teacher's Pet, whom we call Pet for short, and Hannah Banana are the two donkeys. If you've read the first book, you know all about them. If you haven't, I'll introduce them by saying that Pet is a quiet homebody, or at least she was until Hannah arrived. Hannah Banana is a retired circus donkey that came to live with us when she came off the road. She has thoroughly corrupted Pet with her worldly wisdom and mischievous ways.

Also living in the back pastures with the donkeys are Gerald and the Rental Sheep, Stitches, and Jackie. You've already met Gerald and the girls, and they are their own hot mess. Stitches and Jackie are both horses. You might recall that Millie and Clu used to live out there, but they have both gone on to the pasture in the sky. Each of them made it to thirty years old, so they had a good run.

Stitches is a retired brood mare who isn't much of a mom. Her mom wasn't much of a mom either, so it's easy to see why she's lacking the skills and instincts. When Stitches was born, she managed to get her leg stuck under the stall door and injured her hock. She never healed properly, so she looks like she's smuggling a grapefruit in her leg. She can walk just fine, but she was never going to be an athlete. She's not very bright, so it's probably best that she didn't make it as a brood mare, too. Her giant redeeming quality is that she is absolutely fine being at the bottom of the pecking order, and she wants to be friends with every horse she meets. Best friends. While she clearly has some self-worth issues, that fault makes her a great companion horse. So, while she doesn't technically belong to us, she's on permanent loan to the vet clinic. When we have a client who needs a temporary companion horse, Stitches goes wherever she's needed. The rest of the time, she hangs out with Jackie.

Jackie is a retired schooling horse. She's one that I didn't know we owned until Erica and I had been married for a few years. She lived at a training barn, teaching kids how to ride cross rails. She's one of those superhero horses that trainers talk fondly about, the kind of horse who keeps the kid in the saddle and jumps the rail regardless of what's happening. She knew her job, and she loved it. There's no telling how many kids started their riding career on Jackie, but it was a lot. She didn't retire until she was in her twenties, and only then due to lameness issues that took her out of the game. Now she runs the back field.

The back-field crew stays out there around the clock. Gerald and the rental sheep get to move around the farm during the day to weed the other pastures, but the horses and donkeys stay put. Feed time is the big excitement of their day, and a new hay bale showing up is akin to Christmas. Everyone gets excited.

The challenge starts at the gate. I'm by myself when I do this, and I have to open the gate, drive through it, and get back out and close the gate behind me. Sounds simple, right? Wrong. They know when the truck pulls around the barn and starts across the yard what's about to happen, and everyone lines up at the gate.

I try to shoo them back from the gate, open it, then race back to the truck and pull through before they come back to it. Sometimes this works, most times it does not. Stitches and Jackie are tall enough to reach over the side of the truck and start eating hay, so their game plan is to play along while I push them back from the gate, and as soon as I get back in the truck, they rush the gate. I don't think Stitches is as committed to the food as Jackie is, but she wants to do whatever Jackie wants to do, so she's always there, running around like a maniac with no idea why. It's almost never a big deal if they get out the gate before I get in, as they'll just follow the truck and the hay out to the feeder, snatching bites over the side of the bed.

The donkeys, on the other hand, can't reach the hay when it's in the back of the truck. If the tailgate is down and it looks like maybe they can grab a bite, they might follow the truck back into the pasture. Then again, the lure of the great wide open is powerful, and sometimes the urge to run around the farm gets the best of them, and off they go. I've tried a variety of ways of handling this situation, and I've determined that if they take off, it's best to just let them go. By the time I have the hay unloaded, they'll have worked most of it out of their system. All they really want to do is poop in the barn aisle and show off to the horses that they're out and about on their own recognizance.

On this particular day, Gerald and the girls were hanging out in the back pastures when I pulled up with a bale of hay. I pushed them away from the gate where they'd been napping and tried to get the horses and donkeys to move back. With the sheep milling around, there was enough congestion and confusion for me to get the truck through the gate without losing anyone, which is a rare occasion.

I closed the gate, patting myself on the back for my good timing, and opened the truck door. There was a horse on each side of the bed, pulling bits of hay out of the bale, and the donkeys were at the tailgate, eating the loose hay from the bale I'd just unloaded up front. Before I could get my foot up on the running board, a sheep jammed itself between me and the seat, sniffing the floorboard.

"Gerald!" I tried to pull him out of the way, but he had a better angle than I did. I scratched his chest for a moment before picking him up and setting him down out of the way. While I had my back turned, Tweak jumped up in the driver's seat and leaned against the steering wheel, honking the horn.

"Get out of the truck!" I shouted. "What in the world is all this? There are no sheep allowed in the truck, it's Rule #3. We've been over this!"

I couldn't pull her back out of the truck. Sheep are tough to manhandle anyway, but when you have one in the cab of your truck, there's just no room to get the advantage. I went around and opened the passenger door, trying not to think about the mud and poop getting ground into my seat. At least I was in the old truck. If it had been the new truck, I'd have been in heart failure.

Returning to the driver's side, I pushed her through. Finding nothing interesting to chew on, she jumped out willingly enough. I leaned through and closed the passenger door, shaking my head. The sheep do some crazy things sometimes, but this was a first. I put the truck in gear and slowly rolled over to the hay feeder. I thought my troubles were over, but they weren't. Not by a long shot.

I put the truck in reverse and looked in the mirrors. There was still a horse on each side, blocking most of my view, but I could also just make out a donkey butt poking out from behind. I honked the horn and backed up a few inches. Nobody moved except the sheep, who weren't even in the way anymore.

With a deep sigh, I put the truck in park and walked back to push the donkeys out of the way, making sure to close my door. Pet and Hannah were both behind the truck. There was quite a bit of loose hay near the tailgate that they were interested in, so I scooped it up and carried it over to the hay feeder.

"Come on, Pet," I said, showing her the hay. "Come over here." I walked down the side of the hay feeder and put the hay in a pile on the other end. Pet didn't budge.

I jumped up in the air, shouting and waving my arms. "Buaaaahhhhh!" Hannah trotted off a few steps, so I smacked Pet on the rump. She jumped and ran over beside Hannah. This was probably the best that I was going to get, so I ran back to the truck and hopped in. I put in reverse and glanced in the mirrors just in time to see a white donkey butt disappear from view behind the truck. I slumped forward with a sigh.

There didn't seem to be any hope of chasing them off or enticing them away, so I decided to just creep back slowly. I put it in reverse and began inching back. Once they were getting pushed by the tailgate, I thought sure they'd move out of the way. Again, I was wrong.

I could see the hay feeder getting closer in the mirror. The edge of the table is about even with the dropped tailgate, and when I was about three feet away, I stopped and got out again. Both donkeys were behind the truck.

"Go on," I shouted, smacking Hannah on the rump and waving my hands wildly. "Get out of the way!" I closed the tailgate, trying to take away all access to the hay. Stitches ran away, but Hannah just gave me a baleful look. If she was challenging my commitment to our relationship, she was doing a great job of putting the stress on it. "I will drive away and leave you all out here to starve." I don't think they bought the lie. Hannah and Pet stood still, calling my bluff.

Some people might have been tempted to use a whip to chase them away by this time, but I've tried that before. The only thing it got me was a red stripe across my back and a lot of excruciating pain, as I managed to whip my own bare, sweaty back in a colossal whoops moment. I don't even bother with the whip anymore, just for my own safety.

I climbed back in the truck and started creeping back again. At some point the donkeys would start getting penned in, and they would have to move out of the way. The truck inched closer to the feeder. They were just being obstinate now, as there was nothing to eat within reach. I saw the table rock in the mirror, and a moment later Pet shot out the side. One down, one to go. I rolled back another inch.

I couldn't see anything out of the passenger mirror. Stitches had gone around and joined Jackie on that side, and the two of them blocked my view entirely as they munched on the hay. I put the truck in park and jumped out to give Hannah another push. She was standing sideways, parallel with the tailgate. Her ear twitched as I made eye contact with her.

"Alright, Hannah, you win. Whatever kind of willpower contest this is, I concede. You're the champ. You put the 'ass' in 'pain in the ass.' I can't compete. Now then, if you'll step right over here, we'll get your prize."

I swept my arm to the side, going all in on my Bob Barker tangent. To my surprise, Hannah walked out and spun in a circle. I was flabbergasted, but I found enough presence of mind to run over and drop the tailgate before she changed her mind. There was only about six inches of space between the tailgate and the feeder now, so she wasn't going to squeeze back in there. I backed the truck up the rest of the way and shut the motor off.

"I swear," I said, shaking my head as I got out. "I don't even know why I like you all so much. This is a really one-sided relationship."

Pet walked over and turned her butt to me, which is how she makes sure I know right where she wants to be scratched.

"Oh, now you want me to scratch your butt?" I stuck my nose up in the air and stalked to the back of the truck as arrogantly as I could. "I don't even know who you are. I'm just here to deliver hay for the horses. This is hay for critters with manners."

Having had their fun, they went to the other end of the table where I had put the loose hay earlier and began munching on it. I untied the hay net, draped it over the bale, and flipped it over onto the table. After tying the net back to the rafters, I hopped down.

The horses and donkeys were gathered around the hay bale, ignoring me. The sheep had wandered to the other side of the pasture. It had taken me fifteen minutes to drive fifty feet getting in here, and now I could cruise around at thirty miles an hour if I wanted to. I slowly cruised back out to the gate. There was no one there to challenge me, and I drove out and closed it without any pressure at all, a complete reversal of going in.

I decided that if I ever find myself getting annoyed about having to go get the donkeys out of the barn, that I would remember this day. Pushing them back out from the barn is far easier than getting them out of the way had been. However, with each passing minute, I was becoming less irritated and more tickled about the whole thing. It's impossible to stay mad at the donkeys for long. They're just being who they are, with no apologies. Maybe they were trying to help me find a bit of that in myself. God knows I could use some of that.

Chapter 9

A Rough Start to the New Year

IT'S BEEN A LONG TIME SINCE I STAYED UP to see the new year in, and on this New Year's Day I was up before 5:00 am, just like any other day. I sat down at the computer to check all the websites that I manage, before waking Erica up to get her day started. Suddenly, the silence of the sleepy house was shattered by the theme song to National Lampoon's *Christmas Vacation,* which was Erica's current ringtone.

"Hello, Dr. Lacher." Her voice was groggy. She's not a morning person, and I've learned that she sleeps the hardest right before it's time to get up.

There was a long period of silence. I was just starting to think it was a wrong number or something when she spoke again.

"Yep, it sounds like it. Give me a few minutes and I'll be on the way."

I headed for the bedroom to get dressed. I wasn't sure what was going on, but someone was having a rough start to the new year.

"What do we have?" I asked, grabbing my pants off the dresser.

"Colic in Archer, off 241. Cynthia Freeman." She looked at her phone for a moment, squinting past the sleepies in her eyes. "Forty-three degrees. It's freezing outside, I need my fleece."

I know, I know, us Florida people are spoiled. The high for New Year's Day was going to be in the high sixties. We pay for such mild winter temps by sweltering in the heat and humidity during the summertime, which usually lasts from April until November, so don't beat us up too bad for freezing in the forties.

I grabbed a knit watch cap on the way out the door and headed down the stairs. At 5:15 am, the sky was filled with stars, but I didn't have time to do more than glance at them. We raced down the driveway and turned east on Newberry Road.

"Who's up feeding at this time of day?" I asked. "Especially on New Year's, I thought I was the only crazy person up at the crack of dawn."

"Probably her husband," Erica said. "He's a deputy sheriff. Maybe he's working this morning."

That made sense. Holiday or no holiday, there were probably a lot of people working. "What's the story on the horse?"

"Thirty-year-old Arab mare," Erica said, looking at her laptop screen. "Looks like Dr. Russel saw her for a colic a few months ago."

"Uh oh, that's not good."

"No," Erica agreed. "Not at that age."

It only took about fifteen minutes to get there. I turned onto a dirt road and followed it to the end. There was a gate across the drive, and a rustic overhead entrance made from telephone poles. Erica jumped out and opened the gate, closing it behind me. A moment later we passed the house, where a police car was parked, and pulled up to the barn.

The headlights lit up the dark area in front of the barn, where two people stood with a horse. The horse's head was down at her knees, and Erica threw the door open before I even got stopped.

"Grab the lactate meter," she said over her shoulder.

I left the motor running and the lights on and met her at the back of the truck. She grabbed her stethoscope, a syringe, and the thermometer and took off running. I pulled the lactate meter from the bottom left drawer and followed her to the horse. She had already drawn a bit of blood when I got there and handed me the needle. I stuck a test strip in the meter and squeezed a drop of blood on the end of it. She listened to the horse's gut sounds and heartrate while I waited for the result.

"3.9," I announced. A normal, healthy horse has a lactate anywhere between 0.1 and 3.0. It's a measure of the lactic acid in the blood, which increases when something is systemically wrong. For example, a gas colic or mild impaction is systemically fine, so their lactate will be in the normal range, even though they're uncomfortable. A horse with compromised intestine, on the other hand, is not fine, and will have a higher lactate score. It's a good test to determine how serious the colic is in about fifteen seconds.

Erica pulled the stethoscope from her ears. "Her heartrate is well over one hundred. I'm guessing that her lactate would be even higher than that if her circulation was better. Let me grab some pain meds for her, and then we'll make a plan."

We went back to the truck, and I put the lactate meter away as she pulled up a syringe of pain medication.

"What do you think?" I asked. I knew that a regular resting heartrate for a horse was in the thirties, so over one hundred sounded bad.

"Strangulating lipoma, almost guaranteed. We need to euthanize her, but I'm going to give her some pain meds first so we can explain all this to them without making the horse suffer longer. Let's go."

Cynthia was holding the horse and her husband held a flashlight. The horse was incredibly stoic, standing still and calm. Her face gave away the amount of pain she was in, though, with the points and wrinkles around her eyes and nostrils and the position of her ears.

I was surprised that a hot breed like an Arab would be so quiet, but then again, I've heard Erica tell a thousand different people that if the horse isn't acting normal, something is wrong. Of course, horses are prey animals, so it's in their nature to hide pain and distress so that they don't get eaten by a wolf or a tiger, or a plastic bag. Still, most horses with a heartrate that high are throwing themselves on the ground, probably hoping for a tiger to make the pain stop.

"Okay, I'm just going to give her a quick shot," Erica said, squatting down beside the horse's neck. "This will take the edge off for her."

"Okay," Cynthia said.

Erica stood up and handed me the needle. "Okay. Sorry to rush through everything at the outset, but I could tell she was in trouble when we pulled up."

"Oh, nothing to apologize for," Cynthia said. "This is

about Queenie, not us."

Cynthia and her husband were dressed for working out, as if they were headed to the gym. She had to be freezing in her leggings, but she hid it well. Her husband was in workout pants and a thin fleece. They were in their early forties, just like us, but they obviously put us to shame in terms of staying fit. I tried to suck my belly in a bit.

"What's the situation, doc?" her husband asked.

"Oh, I'm sorry," Cynthia said. "Dr. Lacher, this is my husband, Terry."

"No worries," Erica said, shaking his hand. "This is my husband, Justin."

I shook hands with Terry. He had a beard like me, so I forgave him a little for having a flat stomach.

"So, here's the situation," Erica said. "With a heartrate that high, there's only a few things likely to be going on. At her age, it's almost certainly a strangulating lipoma. I can do a full workup on her if you want, but the outcome is going to be the same."

"Is it fixable?" Terry asked.

"Technically." Erica shrugged with a sad smile. "We can send her to surgery, but these guys don't do well post-surgery. And it will likely happen again. They never have just one lipoma. The abdomen wall gets a lot of them hanging down, and they wrap around the intestines and cut off circulation. I wish I had a better answer, but there really isn't a good one."

Terry and Cynthia looked at one another and let out a deep sigh together.

"We were ready to euthanize her the last time she colicked," Cynthia said. "She perked up right at the last second, or she wouldn't be here now."

Terry reached out and patted Queenie on the neck. "Yeah, I don't want to keep putting her through this. I think we call it."

Cynthia wrapped her arms around Queenie's neck and buried her face in her thick winter coat. After a moment, she stepped back, her eyes glistening in the headlights. "Can we bury her here on the farm?"

"Yeah, we can put her out by the fence," Terry said. He glanced at Erica. "Do you know anybody with a backhoe?"

Erica nodded. "Yeah, I can give you a number. If we're going to do that, I'm going to do this a bit differently."

Terry raised his eyebrows in a questioning manner.

"We normally use phenobarbital," Erica said. "It works great, but it leaves a serious residue in the ground, and it lasts a really long time. We don't want that getting in the drinking water. There's a new technique we're just starting to use where we inject lidocaine right into the spinal cavity at the brain. They still go to sleep, but it's a bit slower, and it takes a few minutes for the heart to stop beating. The upside is that the drug residue isn't near as bad."

"Yeah, let's definitely do that," Cynthia said. "We get our water from a well."

"Okay. You get her where you want her, and we'll go get everything ready and meet you there."

We walked to the back of the truck. Erica handed me a bottle of lidocaine and a needle and pointed to the bottom left drawer. "There's two 60cc syringes in there. Put 50cc's of this in each one."

I drew up the drugs while Erica logged it in the controlled drug log. We have to track every drop of controlled drugs, and the paperwork trail is impressive. I added a couple of catheters to the tray, along with her headlamp and the clippers. Erica added a syringe of nerve block for the injection area, and we walked over to the gate beside the barn and entered the back pasture.

"I'm not sure which way they went," I said, peering into the darkness. Sunrise was still an hour away, and it was pitch black in the field.

A flashlight popped on to our left, and Terry jogged over to us. "We're going to do it over there by the fence."

He swung the light around, and the beam lit up a cow and two young calves. Their eyes reflected the flashlight in a dazzling yellow flash.

"Aw, you've got adorable baby cows," Erica said.

Terry laughed. "Yeah, their mom over there is Daisy, and they're Mike and Ike." He swung the light around in a slow circle. "There's a bull out here, somewhere."

"Oh, boy," I muttered.

Terry laughed. "Don't worry, he's friendly. They're all practically pets."

He walked over to Queenie, lighting the way for us. They were about fifty yards away from the barn, near an old tree by the fence. "Cynthia's mom and dad are on their way over," he said as he walked. "They live right around the corner, so they'll be here in just a minute."

"Okay, no worries." Erica stopped beside Queenie and scratched her ears. "She's had a pretty fantastic run. You'd never know she was thirty to look at her."

Cynthia smiled as she wiped her eyes. "She's been my horse since she was four. We got her the summer I turned 14. My folks have hauled her to a thousand horse shows, so I thought I owed it to them to let them be here to tell her goodbye."

"What was your sport?" I asked.

"We did Arab shows," she said, reaching out to rub Queenie's neck. "She was my Arab hunter. Do you remember those days, girl? We had a lot of good times."

Terry put his arm around Cynthia's shoulders and gave her a squeeze, and I looked away. Every time I attend an end-of-life event, I'm humbled by the history that people share with their horses. It also makes me feel a little hollow. I never had a horse of my own. For that matter, I don't think I've had anything for thirty years, much less another life form that I had such a bond with. When I get a glimpse of what I missed out on, it hurts in a weird way. I don't want to call it jealousy, because that makes it seem petty. It's more than that. I think I grieve for something I never had, a connection that I craved all the way up until I met Erica. I hope people who do get to have that experience can appreciate it.

"Come on, Dad," Terry said. "It's only a thirty-second drive."

I chuckled. "Maybe he didn't know you meant right this minute. He could be making coffee."

"Knowing my dad, he's cooking bacon and eggs," Cynthia said. She tucked her chin and dropped her voice, obviously imitating him. "You can't start the day without a good breakfast."

Terry laughed with delight. "That's him to a T."

A branch snapped nearby, and Terry turned the flashlight on, sweeping it in a slow arc. The cows were closer now, blinking against the glare. Another horse was nearby as well, grazing on the low grass.

"They're like the Weeping Angels from Dr. Who," I said to Erica. "Every time the light goes out, they get closer."

"Don't blink," she whispered back.

Terry shut the light off, then turned it back on a few

seconds later. The cows were even closer. "I think you're right," he said. "They're going to be in our pocket here in a minute. Old Pete's finally making an appearance, too."

"He looks incredible," Erica said. "How old is he now? He's older than Queenie, right?"

"He's five years older than her," Terry said. "Thirty-five, I guess."

I was surprised at that. Old Pete was a body condition score of five, maybe even six. That's rare in a horse that age.

Headlights lit up the trees out front, and a car pulled up to the gate. A moment later it parked by the barn, and Terry walked over to guide them across the field.

As they approached, the cows shifted around beside us. The two calves walked up beside Queenie, then bucked and scampered off a few steps as Cynthia's mom walked up to Queenie and hugged her neck.

"Oh, Queenie girl, I'm so sorry," she said, her voice catching. Her husband put an arm around her, and the other around Queenie's neck. Cynthia and Terry stepped up, and the five of them stood there a moment in a group hug. Erica and I stood back, giving them some time to say goodbye.

The stars were starting to fade as light crept into the eastern sky, but I could still spot a few of my favorite constellations. I stared at them for a minute, trying to find a connection between the endless energy of the life cycle here on earth and the vast and strange energy of the cosmos, always changing, always moving. Erica nudged me, and I returned my focus to Queenie and her family.

The cows were back, closer than ever. As dawn approached, I could make out the shape of the calves, Mike and Ike. They stood by Queenie's flanks, staring at the spectacle of the people hugging the horse. It dawned on me that Queenie had been a staple in their lives too, right from day one. Granted, that was only a month or two ago for them, but that didn't make it any less important.

"Okay," Cynthia said at last, stepping back. "We need to do this. The pain meds are going to wear off."

"You were the best horse there ever was," Cynthia's mom said. "Thank you for taking care of my baby all these years."

Cynthia burst into tears. "Thank you for being my best friend." She hugged Queenie again. "Okay, Dr. Lacher."

Erica and I moved up to Queenie. I held the tray, and she switched on her headlamp. "I'm going to sedate her first," she said. "She's going to get sleepy, and I'll give her another drug that will anesthetize her. She'll fall down, and then we'll give the lidocaine. Once I tell you it's safe, you can come back up and spend her last few minutes with her, okay?"

They nodded, shuffling back a few steps.

"Son, let's push these cows back," Cynthia's dad said. Terry flicked his light on and chuckled.

"They can't stand not being in the middle of something." They walked towards the cows, shooing them back towards the barn. Old Pete still stood where he'd been, watching and eating.

Erica gave the first shot. I held the tray with one hand, and scratched Queenie's neck with the lead rope. "That's a good girl," I whispered. "It's going to be okay."

After a minute, her head hung even lower, and Erica squatted down, giving her the anesthetic. She put the needle in the tray, and I stepped back, handing her the lead rope. Queenie swayed back and forth a few times before her knees buckled. Erica was ready and shoved her back on her haunches. She rolled onto her left side, and Erica gently eased her head to the ground. As soon as they were still, I moved back up beside Erica, behind Queenie.

"Let's get her halter off," Erica said. I put the tray down and slipped around Erica. I lifted Queenie's head, and Erica unclipped the chin strap, working the halter down around my hands. When it was off, I set her head down as easy as I could. Queenie let out a deep sigh but didn't move.

"I need you to draw her nose in towards her chest," Erica said.

This was my first time doing a euthanasia like this, and I wasn't really sure of my role. Erica is a patient teacher, so I knew she would guide me where she needed me, but I still wished I had gone through the procedures with her beforehand. Nothing eats at my insecurities like not knowing what I'm doing. I squatted down, pulling Queenie's head in slowly. "Say when."

"That's good, hold it there."

Erica took the clippers and trimmed a small square on the back of Queenie's head, shaving the hair down to the skin. She inserted a catheter at the top of Queenie's spine, at the base of her skull. Clear fluid streamed out, and she quickly stuck a large syringe on the catheter and drew out 20cc's of spinal fluid. She emptied it onto the ground and repeated the process a few more times.

"We're making space," she said softly, as she emptied the syringe a second time. "If we force the lidocaine in without removing some of the spinal fluid, it puts a lot of pressure in there. It will still achieve the goal, but it would be painful for her, and we don't want that."

"No, she's already in enough pain," Cynthia said. "Thank you for doing that."

With some of the spinal fluid removed, Erica quickly

injected the lidocaine. She emptied the first syringe, pulled it off the needle, and jammed the second one on, pressing the plunger down firmly. When it was empty, she pulled the catheter out, holding her finger firmly over the injection site. I took the syringes and picked up the tray, backing out of the way so the family could come back up.

Everyone gathered around Queenie, stroking her neck. As often happens in these moments, they began telling stories about various Queenie experiences. This is one of the things I treasure most about my job.

"Do you remember the time when Queenie bucked you off at Nationals?" Cynthia's mom asked. "I think you were 15 or 16."

"Oh, my god," Cynthia burst into gales of laughter, tears still streaming from her eyes. "I was so embarrassed! I swore I'd never ride in public again, remember?"

"Oh, yes, we spent weeks talking you off the ledge after that."

"Talk about a long ride home," her dad said. "Sixteen hours with three people in the truck, and the only time anybody said anything was when you needed a bathroom break!"

"How about the time she unhooked both gates and was grazing out by the highway," Terry said. "I was still new on the squad back then, and I remember our neighbor's address coming across the radio, and a description of a black horse on the side of 241. That took about ten years off my life."

"Oh, yeah, I had forgotten about that," Cynthia exclaimed. "You were way out on the other side of the county, and I was at work when you called, and mom wouldn't answer the phone, and we didn't know what to do. I could have killed her that day."

"I was out on the highway chasing Queenie!" her mom

protested. "Me and Janice Miles out there in our bathrobes with two deputies, trying to corner an ornery horse."

"Well, I didn't know that at the time. I don't think we even had cellphones back then."

"You had me at the hardware store trying to buy chains and padlocks, and I didn't even know what size they needed to be," her mother said. "Wow, that was a day. Thank god the neighbors saw her out the window and got her back on the dirt road before she got hit."

Erica slipped her stethoscope into her ears and listened for a heartbeat. They turned to her as one as she took it back off and draped it around her neck. "She's gone. Her heart's still beating slowly, but that's the last thing to stop." She patted Queenie's side. "It sounds like she taught you some life lessons."

Cynthia shook her head. "A million times. I think she taught me everything I know, one way or another."

"That's what horses do," Erica said. "Isn't that right, Mike? Or are you Ike?"

I stepped back so I could see past the people. The cows were back, all four of them this time. Old Pete was even making his way over, sniffing the air cautiously. I had seen lots of horses and donkeys coming to say goodbye at times like these, and even dogs and cats on occasion, but never cows. I felt unprofessional laughing about it, so I kept my chuckles to myself, but it was funny to see. Now that it was getting light, I could see the calves more clearly. They were light brown with big white splotches across their faces, and they were absolutely adorable. They reminded me of Gerald and the rental sheep with their inquisitiveness and cuteness. There's just something about baby animals. Baby people don't really do it for me, but I could watch babies of most other species all day long.

Erica checked Queenie's vitals and pupil reaction, confirming that everything was as it should be. "Okay," she said, standing up. "Her heart stopped. You guys gave her a wonderful life. A lot of horses don't get that, and I appreciate what you've done for her."

Cynthia walked over and wrapped her arms around Erica, hugging her close. "Thank you for this," she whispered fiercely. "Thank you."

We made our way slowly back to the truck. Erica typed everything up in the computer while I put the stuff away and cleaned up the trash. The family stood nearby, continuing to tell stories about Queenie. Terry came over when Erica was finished and handed her a credit card.

"We're starting the New Year off with a bang," he said. "I thought it was going to be a quiet one for a change, since I was off work."

"You can't win," I said. "We have the same problem. Between the horses, donkeys, sheep, cats and dogs, somebody is always willing to throw a wrench in the plans."

"Oh, we used to have sheep," Terry said with a laugh. "That's a whole different set of problems. They ate everything on the property."

"Here you go," Erica said, returning his card and handing him a sheet of paper. "I wrote the phone number on there for the backhoe guy. He's really great. His daughter is a crazy horse girl, so he understands us."

Terry folded the paper and slipped it in his pocket. "Thanks again, we really appreciate everything. Sorry to ruin your New Year's Day morning."

"You didn't ruin anything," Erica said. "This is what we do."

We shook hands again and drove away. The sun was just

cresting on the horizon, turning the few stray wispy clouds over-head a bright pink. By the time we got home, it was nearly time to feed our horses. I gave them each an extra pat on the neck as we brought them in, and I stood out back with the donkeys for a few minutes, scratching their backs and giving them fusses. It's easy to take them all for granted when everything's going fine, but watching someone else lose a horse always reminds me to appreciate ours more intentionally. Gerald came over while I was playing with the donkeys and poked his head under my arm.

"Alright, alright," I said, dropping down to one knee. "I'll give you a chest scratch."

The rest of the day was quiet. I got a lot of writing done in the morning, and spent some time with Erica after she finished riding Ernie and Vespa. I think we were both feeling grateful for what we have. Our lives are surrounded by all kinds of animals, and that's the way we like it. Doing what we do for a living helps us appreciate them, because we're constantly reminded that it's temporary. Sometimes it's a hard lifestyle, but I wouldn't trade it for anything.

Chapter 10

VISITING HIGHWAY

IF YOU'VE READ THE PREVIOUS BOOK in this series, then you're familiar with Highway, the I-75 Miracle Horse. If you haven't read that one, or if you've forgotten who he is, I'll give a brief introduction to him, just to get you up to speed.

Highway, as we named him, was a barrel racing quarter horse who cracked under the stress associated with going in the arena to perform. He was okay for years, but at some point, he just couldn't do it anymore. When that happened, he would lose his mind when it was time to run, and he would take off in the wrong direction, trying to get away from it. This caused him to be sold, and the person who bought him thought she could "fix" him.

When it became clear that he wasn't going to be a barrel racer anymore, his last owner decided to euthanize him since he couldn't perform. She claimed it was so no one would get hurt on him because he was dangerous, but I guess it was never an option for him to retire or do something besides compete. She didn't want to spend the money to have him euthanized, so she found a guy who would supposedly kill the horse for free. I'll bite my tongue on how I feel about that, just to avoid being aggressive and judgmental. Anyway, what really happened was that she gave the horse to a guy who was going to take him to a slaughter auction.

Early on the fateful morning of November 30th, 2018, this guy loaded several horses on his trailer and set off up I-75. For some reason, he pulled over on the shoulder just south of Paynes Prairie, near Micanopy, Florida. When he took off again, the trailer door came open. Highway, who was the last horse on the trailer, made a decision that should have killed him, but turned out to be the best thing he could have done: he jumped off the trailer.

There are a hundred different things that might have happened. There might have been a tractor trailer behind them that couldn't stop in time. He might have fallen in a way that killed him or broke a bunch of bones. He might have gone through the windshield of a car and killed a bunch of people. Fortunately for Highway, none of those things happened. When he hit the pavement, he fell to his knees, sliding down the asphalt. The injuries to his knees were severe, and the pain had to have been unbelievable. He fell over on his side, still sliding down the road. He rolled up on his withers, leaving a trail of road rash across his side and shoulder. As the trailer dwindled into the distance, never slowing, he forced himself to his feet and staggered to the side of the interstate. He stood there in the ditch in the pre-dawn darkness, suffering greatly, but alive.

The sheriff's department called us, and we went out and picked him up off the side of the road. His knee joints were packed with asphalt, and he was covered in scrapes and abrasions, but he was bright-eyed and engaged. We got him back to the clinic and cleaned him up, but he needed surgery fast if he was going to live. He was very friendly and interactive, so no one wanted to consider euthanizing him.

Lacking an owner, we did a GoFundMe campaign to raise the money for it. People from all over the world chipped in, and we raised $10,000 in a day. Highway went to Ocala, Florida, to a referral hospital, where they removed the asphalt and flushed his joints. We brought him to our house to recover, and he stayed there for about a month before going to a rescue facility that would become his forever home.

That's the condensed version of what happened. If you'd like to read the full story, it's Chapter 7 of the first book in this series, *Adventures of the Horse Doctor's Husband*.

We did a good job of making Highway a celebrity, and he developed a large following both in person and on Facebook. As the feature story of the first book, a portion of the proceeds have gone to Dreamcatcher Ranch Rescue to help support his ongoing care. We've also attended some local events to sell books and raise money for him, and in November, 2019, he attended an event with us.

It was the annual Three-Day Event at the Ocala Jockey Club. If you're not familiar with it, it's a big deal. This horse show is an Olympic qualifying event, so all the best of the best eventers were in attendance.

Three-day eventing is an interesting sport. If you don't

know what it is, I'll give you my outsider's limited understanding of it. This sport combines dressage, show jumping, and cross-country riding. It requires a wide range of skill for the rider and the horse, as well as an incredible level of fitness and endurance. Some people think it also requires a certain level of madness, at least on the cross-country part, and I have a hard time arguing with that. The cross-country course is about fourteen minutes of galloping around a massive course, jumping the biggest, most terrifying things you can imagine. There are huge tree trunks, trenches, big slabs of wood, and even some where you jump through a screen of bushes into a pond.

This event generally draws a huge crowd of thousands of people, and as supporters of Highway, the event organizers invited us to come set up a table and sell books. They set up a place for Highway so that people could come meet him, and he got a fifteen-minute spot in the main arena so that we could tell people about him. It was a wonderful opportunity, and we gratefully accepted.

When the weekend finally arrived, Erica and I loaded up our canopy, table, and several boxes of books. The weather was cold and drizzly, but the forecast said it was going to clear off and get sunny. I don't know why, but I believed it.

We were scheduled to be there Friday through Sunday, but Highway was only coming over on Saturday. We didn't want to stress him out by pulling him from his quiet existence among friends at the rescue and put him in the high-energy environment of a major horse show for three days. A few hours would be plenty.

The Ocala Jockey Club is a stunningly beautiful property, with rolling hills and clumps of massive live oaks scattered here and there. On a clear day, you can stand outside the clubhouse and see several of the huge cross-country obstacles in the distance in every direction. That day, you could see about three hundred yards. It was just dismal.

On Friday, Erica and I sat at the table and froze our butts off. The weather said it was fifty degrees Fahrenheit, but there was a cold wind blowing, and the mist never cleared up. We had jackets, but they were light, and didn't do anything to stop the wind from cutting through us. By noon, our feet were frozen, and we were both sporting snotcicles on our red noses. We abandoned our efforts to look professional and strung up a tarp across the back of the booth to try to keep the books dry. It blocked some of the wind, too, so that was good.

Because of the weather, very few spectators showed up. I couldn't blame them; I didn't want to be there, either. We sold a few books, but we spent more money on coffee and giant hot pretzels than we made. On the upside, we had a great view of the arena where the dressage and show jumping was happening, and Erica knew who some of the people were. It was neat getting to see people who were celebrities in the horse world ride some of the finest horses in the world.

On Saturday, we made better decisions.

"The weather says it's supposed to clear off," Erica said. We were down in the barn, bringing the horses in before breakfast. It was in the low forties, and still misty and foul.

"That's what they said yesterday," I said. "It never happened. I think we ought to take a thermos full of hot tea, raincoats, and gloves. I froze yesterday, and I don't want to go through that again."

"Agreed." As soon as we got upstairs, Erica put a kettle on to boil, and I texted Loran, who owns the rescue where

Highway lives now, to let her know to dress warm.

We're set up near the top of a hill. It's cold and windy, and very damp. You'll want to bring a coat and a hat. We froze yesterday!

Her reply came a few minutes later. *Thanks for the heads up! Highway just got a new waterproof sheet with his name embroidered on it, and it looks like we might need it.*

Perfect timing! I replied. *See you in a few hours.*

We were sitting in our booth, huddled over a cup of tea, when Loran and her mom, Allie, arrived with Highway. I had seen him at the rescue facility a few months before when we did the photo shoot for the cover of the first book, but Erica hadn't seen him in nearly a year. A huge grin spread across her face as he stepped off the trailer.

"Highway! You look incredible!" Erica scratched his neck as she looked him over. I knew what she was seeing, as I had gone through the same process in August. Highway is nearly jet black, especially when he has his winter coat. Every place that he had an abrasion from sliding down the interstate was now marked with white hair. There was a white stripe on his cheek, a big spot on his withers, down his shoulder and ribs, his flank, and of course, his knees. He was in fantastic condition, but seeing the symbols of so many injuries was enough to bring tears to my eyes. He knickered softly, as he did every time we walked into the barn back when he stayed with us.

"I think he remembers you," Loran said. She stuck out her hand. "It's weird to meet you in person, since I've known you for a year, but I'm Loran."

Erica laughed. "I know! I've talked to you on the phone, texted, emailed, and here we are, finally face to face."

"This is my mom, Allie," Loran said. "Mom, this is Dr. Lacher."

"Hi, nice to meet you," Allie said. She had a charming British accent, and a sensible hat and scarf covering most of her curly blond hair. "Thank you for saving Highway. He's really changed our world."

"Thank you for giving him a safe place to live," Erica said. "He's had a rough ride, and he needed somebody to love him no matter what."

Loran rubbed his muzzle. "I've got a lot of horses, but I've never bonded with one as tight as we've bonded. We were just meant for each other."

Highway knickered again and dropped his head down to sample the grass. Loran pointed at the portable panels and tugged gently on the lead rope. "You want to go in there so we can get set up? I'll get your hay net out, but I need both hands."

Highway looked up for a moment, his ears pricked, then bent down for another bite of grass. I was nervous, unsure of how he would react to being here. It was very different from a barrel race in most ways, but it was still a horse show. There was a lot of energy in the air, and a lot of horses in the vicinity. So far, though, so good. Loran tugged on the lead rope again, and he followed her into the small pen. As soon as she stepped out and closed the gate, he turned around and backed up against the fence with his tail towards us.

"I'm not scratching your butt right now," Loran said. "I've got work to do."

Highway knickered, looking over his shoulder at her. He obviously had her trained. Loran sighed and scratched his butt, but only for a second.

"I can't believe how good he's moving," Erica said. "He's barely even lame on the bad knee."

Loran smiled. "He's on a very strict exercise schedule, and he gets physical therapy and laser treatments once a week. Dr. Susan thinks he might be sound enough to cut back on some of it by the end of the year."

"You're a testament to following through with the treatment," I said. "He's obviously eating well, too. He's in great shape."

Allie chuckled. "It's hard, sometimes. He gets a lot of people coming out to see him, and everyone wants to give him a bag of carrots, or a treat. We have to keep that under control, or he'd swell up like a blimp!"

We laughed. I felt a little bit guilty, since I wrote about his fondness for carrots. I resolved to do better the next time I wrote about him, and so that moment is now: Highway loves a carrot, but he doesn't need a whole bag of them at a time! One or two baby carrots is an appropriate treat, especially if there are a lot of other people there to see him, too. Moderation in all things!

The crowd was sparse with the weather being so bleak, so Loran put Highway's new personalized sheet on him and walked around the area with him. They got a fair amount of attention and posed for a lot of pictures. We had a steady trickle of people coming through to get a copy of the book, and since I had dressed more appropriately, I was warm enough to sign a legible autograph.

After lunch, I poured the last of the tea into my cup and was warming my hands with it when a group of people walked into our booth. I didn't recognize the woman in front, but I certainly recognized the younger man next to her. It was Tik Maynard.

Tik is also an author, and a very well-known and respected

horse trainer in the eventing world. It turned out that the woman in front of him was his mother, down from Canada to see her son and his wife, who is a highly respected horse trainer and international competitor in her own right. His mom and dad were also famous people in the horse world. I wasn't just meeting a celebrity; I was meeting a celebrity family!

"Hi, I'm Jen Maynard," she said, extending her hand. "We're so glad to meet you!"

I was flabbergasted, and jerked clumsily to my feet, grasping her hand. "I'm Justin Long. Thank you, it's wonderful to meet you. This is my wife, Dr. Erica Lacher." I don't know if I was more nervous that I was meeting famous people, or more surprised that they knew who I was, or had at least heard of my book.

Tik stuck his hand out next, a big smile on his face. "Tik Maynard. Good to meet you."

Once we had made introductions all around, Mrs. Maynard bought a copy of my book. Tik and I immediately fell into a conversation about books and writing. Within minutes, I felt like I'd known him for years.

After our initial meeting, I went over to the booth where Tik was doing his book signing, and talked with him for half an hour. It occurred to me that in a way, the bad weather was a blessing. Had it been nice, there would be too many people there for Tik and me to spend that time together. I liked him immensely, and that made the bad weather much more bearable.

Shortly after that, Loran decided to take Highway back home. He'd been there for nearly six hours, and he was starting to get restless. We all agreed that he'd had a pretty full day.

"Don't forget about Highway's birthday party on the 30th," Loran said, closing the trailer door and latching it. I found myself double-checking the latch, as I have ever since Highway's appearance in our lives. "Hopefully the weather will be nicer than this!"

"We'll be there," I promised. "Erica's on call, but Amy, our office manager, is coming down with me."

"Oh, great!" Loran said. "She's another one I've talked to a lot, but never met."

We shared hugs all around, and they drove away.

Amy and I went down to Clermont a few weeks later. I was excited about the event, because we had already managed to raise $1,000 for Highway through book sales. We had a big check made at our local print shop, and we displayed it on the table so that people could see that their book purchase was really making a difference for Highway.

We went back down there a few weeks later for Dreamcatcher Ranch Rescue's annual Christmas party. This was a completely different crowd, mostly parents bringing their young kids out to feed donkeys and horses, take pony rides, and spend the day on a farm. It was a lot of fun, and I was overwhelmed by the number of people who came by to tell me that they had already read the book and loved it. Highway had a lot of fans in attendance that day!

On the long ride home that evening, Amy and I talked about a variety of things, but the topic always returned to Highway.

"I just can't believe how well he interacts with all the people," Amy said at one point. "He probably had a hundred kids trying to pet his nose today, and he was just as patient as he could be."

"I can't believe he kept his head stuck out his door the whole time," I said. "I would have been hiding back in the corner of the stall."

Amy laughed. "Even when he was out walking around, you'd think he spent his whole life in a petting zoo. He's a natural at this stuff."

"As evidenced by his elf hat," I added. "I don't think any of our horses would have kept that hat on for more than a minute. He had it on all day."

"And the ribbons in his mane and tail," Amy said. "He didn't seem like a dangerous horse that needs to be euthanized for the safety of everyone around him."

"Right?" I agreed. "He didn't need to be thrown away; he just needed a career change."

I'm not going to get into the politics of sending horses to slaughter. I will say, however, that there are tons of horses out there that need a new home, and there are tons of people looking for an affordable horse. It just seems to me that those two problems could solve themselves with a little coordination. Not every one of them will work out as well as it did for Highway, but that doesn't mean they shouldn't get a second chance at life. Hell, I wouldn't be where I am if I didn't get a chance to start over. I'm guessing a lot of people could say the same.

Chapter 11

JUST FOLLOW MY NOSE

HORSES POOP A LOT. Even though I live with seven of them and spend an inordinate amount of my time dealing with their poop in some way, I still occasionally find myself impressed by how much poop they produce. One of my jokes with the feed store people is that horse people have perfected the art of turning money into poop. It's like alchemy, but backwards.

We compost the poop that happens in the stalls during the day, so I can tell you with a high degree of accuracy that those five horses produce about two hundred cubic feet of poop every four weeks, and that's just their daytime poop. The nighttime poop out in the pasture is a little harder to measure. Instead of composting that, we drag it. This breaks it up into smaller particles which will break down faster. It also exposes any parasites in their poop to the heat and sunlight, which kills them off, so they don't spread.

One day I was cruising around the back field, spreading poop. We have a little old lawn tractor from the 1970's that we use to drag pastures. We also use it to pull the manure spreader when we empty the compost bins. It goes about three miles an hour, which is plenty, given the rough terrain. I had my headphones on, listening to a podcast. It's a great way to make the best use of the time, if you like learning things as much as I do.

I was zoned out, listening to an organizational psychologist discussing what makes great teams function so well. At some point, I became aware of a flickering in my peripheral vision, and it finally dawned on me that Erica was parked at the gate in the vet truck, flashing the headlights at me. I swung the tractor towards the gate, but then thought better of it. It would be faster to just walk over, so I shut it off and jogged to the gate.

"Hey," I said, pulling off my headphones as I opened the passenger door. "Do we have an emergency?"

"Yep." She put the truck into gear and spun around. "It's just across the street at Amelia's house."

I put my seatbelt on. "I hope you haven't been sitting here long."

"Nah. I figured you couldn't hear me honking the horn, but you came over as soon as I flashed the lights."

"What's going on at Amelia's?" I asked.

"Musique tried to rip her nose off, and partially succeeded."

I tried to place the name with a face. I'd been to Amelia's farm before, but it takes a lot of repeated exposure for me to remember which horse is which. Erica has a knack for that. I do not, it seems.

"That's the older red mare, right? With the blond mane?"

Erica laughed, shaking her head. "Oh, my god. Yes, but you can't say it like that, especially not in front of horse people."

"Yellow mane? I know 'blond' isn't the proper terminology, but I'm drawing a blank. What do you call yellow in horse-speak?"

"She's a liver chestnut with a flaxen mane," Erica said, rolling her eyes as if I should know these things.

"Okay, I got it. Musique is the Cobb pony with a liver chestnut paintjob and a flaxen mane."

"Welsh."

"What?"

"She's a Welsh pony, not a Cobb."

I shook my head. "Alright, alright, I give up. This is too complicated." We were already pulling down their driveway anyway, so it was time to get to work. Erica pulled the truck around back to the barn, and we hopped out. It was weird for me to climb out the passenger side, as I almost always drive, but I managed to find the door handle and point myself the right way.

"Hey, Dr. Lacher," Amelia called. She was standing in the aisle with her husband, James. "Thanks for getting here so quick. I hope I didn't mess up your weekend."

James and I had gone out riding motorcycles several times in the past, and we get along famously. As Amelia was explaining everything to Erica, James caught my eye and tilted his head toward the stall, and the smirk on his face caused me to chuckle. He didn't need to say anything. I knew what he meant: horses.

I stayed outside the stall as Erica went in to examine Musique, ready to run back to the truck if she needed something. Musique backed away from Erica, a string of blood trailing from her nose to the floor in front of her.

"I can't imagine where she would have cut herself," Amelia was saying. "We've been all over the place trying to find something sharp, but there's no nails sticking out of the fence, no broken water bucket, nothing."

"That's horses," Erica said, putting a hand on Musique's neck. "You could put them in a bubble wrap room, and they'd still find a way to hurt themselves."

She bent forward, squinting as she stared at the bloody muzzle before her. The horse's left nostril was torn in a jagged semicircle, and her whole muzzle was red on that side. The other side was mostly gray from old age.

"You did a number on yourself, kiddo," Erica said. "But that'll heal fine."

Amelia's hands went to her red hair, tightening the ponytail in frustration. "This horse is trying to kill me! First it was a colic, then it was an abscess, and now this. That's enough stress for one year!"

"She's exhibiting all the classic symptoms of a kid that's dying for attention," I said. "She needs to be the star."

James burst out laughing. "That ship has sailed, man. She's a hundred years old."

Amelia gave him a mock frown. "Oh, she is not, don't you say that to her."

"She's got to be, what, twenty-five years old? Thirty?"

Amelia frowned, tilting her head back for a moment as she counted. "I guess she's thirty-one, but we don't talk about it. It makes me feel old."

Erica walked out of the stall and beckoned to me. "Come on, let's go hide behind the vet truck while they hash this out."

I opened the liftgate and pulled the tray out as Erica began drawing up a syringe of nerve block. I grabbed two suture packs, the clippers, scrub, and lube, and jammed a hand towel in my pocket.

"What am I forgetting?" I asked.

Erica capped the needle and put it in the tray, glancing over the other items I'd put there. "I think that'll get us started. I'll just push the needle through the thick horse skin with my poor fingers, I guess."

"Needle drivers! I knew I was forgetting something important." I opened the center drawer and pulled out the instrument pack. "Needle drivers, tweezers, and scissors, right?"

"Forceps."

"Forceps. We're using forceps on the liver chestnut Welsh horse with a flaxen mane."

"Pony."

"I'm never going to learn all this," I said, grinning in spite of myself. "I think you have to start learning it when you're two in order to get it all straight."

"Well, that certainly makes it easier," Erica said. "But you're doing pretty good for an old guy."

"Alright, alright, none of that," I said, bumping her hip with mine. "You've got work to do. Let's go sew up this red and blond pony."

Amelia and James stepped away from the stall door as we walked back over. James opened the door and pulled a halter off the rack, holding it out to Erica. "What do you think, doc? Is she going to make it?"

"It's looking pretty good," Erica said. "But I can't put a halter on her while her nose is ripped in half."

James snorted. "Well, yeah, I guess not, huh?"

A frown of concern crossed Amelia's face. "How are you going to manage her? She might not stand still. As you well know, she can be opinionated sometimes."

"That's what we have drugs for," Erica said, grabbing a needle out of the tray. "And husbands."

I set the tray on top of the water bucket and waited for Erica to give Musique a shot of sedation. As Erica approached her, Musique backed up to the corner and followed the wall around. I reached out and put a hand on her flank as she backed into the corner in front of me, keeping my body back out of kicking range.

"Do you want me to manage her head, or stay right here?" I asked.

Erica stuck the capped needle in her pocket and put a hand on Musique's neck, scratching her withers with the other hand. "Easy, girl. Let me get this shot into you, it'll make you feel better." She glanced at me as she pulled the needle back out of her pocket. "Stay right there for now."

Erica clamped her thumb down on the vein in Musique's neck, and readied the needle. Musique tossed her head a few times, snorting loudly.

"She hates to get a shot," Amelia said. "Are you sure you don't want a lead rope or something to put around her neck? She's being very naughty about all of this."

"I'll take a lead rope," I said. "I might need to rappel out the window before this is over."

It took a minute, but Erica finally got the shot into the horse. We stepped back to give her some space while we waited for the drugs to kick in.

"I need to hose off the laceration," Erica said. "Do you want to do that in here, or out there?"

Amelia glanced around. "Let's do that in the aisle, if you don't mind."

Erica grabbed the lead rope from me and slipped it around Musique's neck. "Come on, kiddo. Let's get you out here before you don't want to move anymore."

The steering wasn't great, nor were the brakes, but we got Musique out into the aisle and stopped. James brought the water hose over and handed it to me, then went back to the faucet. "How much should I turn it on?"

"Not a lot," I said. "About the same as if you were trying to drink out of it."

He slowly turned the handle, and I moved over beside the horse's shoulder, holding the hose beside her head so the water ran down her face without splashing in her eyes. Despite my efforts to be accommodating, Musique didn't think much of it. She shook her head repeatedly, spraying us all with bloody droplets. I kept one hand on her jaw to keep her from leaving, and kept the water coming.

"Alright, let's see what we've got," Erica said. James shut the hose off.

A flap of skin the size and shape of my thumb was torn away, starting at the lip and going to the center of her nose. The outside wall of the nostril was completely separated from her face. The exposed tissue was bright red, but no longer bleeding.

"Oh, my goodness, I haven't even called Doris," Amelia said, patting her pockets in search of her phone. "Her horse is standing here with her nose ripped off, and she doesn't even know." She located her phone and walked out the barn door.

I glanced at Erica with my eyebrows raised. "Musique belongs to Doris?" Erica nodded. Doris was the next-door neighbor, and when I thought about it, it all made sense. Doris had a lot of horses, and they're all ponies. Amelia's other two horses were both big warmbloods, and one of them had only recently arrived. Musique was here as a companion horse. I was disappointed that I hadn't figured that out on my own.

"Let's get her blocked," Erica said.

Musique's head was drooping. I reached back in the stall, grabbed the tray, and set it on the nearby shelf as Erica pulled on a pair of disposable gloves. When she was ready, I handed her the syringe. I went around to the opposite side, put my hands under Musique's jaw and lifted her head up to a comfortable working height for Erica.

Musique was happy to let me support her weight. I've learned through experience that sedated horses will lean on you as long as you're willing to hold them up, and I don't have what it takes to hold a horse up for long. My back starts to ache, my legs get shaky, and the horse gets unstable. My trick to combat this is to drop my arms a fraction every minute or two, which causes them to re-engage and hold their own head up.

The second Musique noticed the needle in Erica's hand coming towards her nose, I no longer had to worry about holding her head up. In fact, my new job became to hold her head down. Being sedated did nothing to dull her distaste for needles. I put a hand on top of her nose up high, and the other on top of her head. She jerked and twisted, making it impossible for Erica to even get started.

"Let's reposition you," Erica said to me. "Reach under her jaw and up this side and grab her ear. Don't yank on it, just hold it firm. That should keep her from jerking her head up."

I got into position. It was a little awkward because I'm so tall and Musique is so short, but I spread my legs wide and made it work. I put my other hand on the bridge of her nose.

"You look like a pro wrestler," James said. "Like you're about to do a crazy takedown move."

I laughed. "I feel like I'm on the other end of that, like she's going to toss her head and throw me up in the rafters."

Erica put her shoulder against Musique's face so she couldn't see the needle coming. At first, it seemed to work. She injected nerve block all around the wound so Musique wouldn't feel the sutures going in. Musique twitched a few times, but she mostly just rested her weight on my shoulder.

When the block was done, Erica grabbed the needle drivers and a suture pack. This is where the real trouble started. There was no way for Erica to block Musique's view and still be able to sew. The angles were all wrong. As soon as she approached with the needle, Musique would toss her head and back up. Sedation, shmedation. Musique wasn't having it.

"Do you want me to block her view?" Amelia asked. "That seemed to work before."

"Let's give it a shot," Erica said. "This certainly isn't working."

I stayed where I was, and Amelia stepped up right in front of me and put her arm across Musique's face.

As soon as Erica grabbed the hanging flap of nostril with her forceps, Musique tossed her head, nearly lifting me off the floor. She snorted, dipped her head in an effort to dislodge me, and shook her head violently.

"Okay, this isn't working," Erica said. "You can let her go."

"Musique, are you being a naughty girl?" We turned to see Doris walking up the aisleway. There was a twinkle in her eye, as there always is when it comes to her ponies.

"Oh, Doris, she's being terrible," Amelia said. "That's how we know she's not hurt too bad. She's being her usual spunky self."

"I know this is ridiculous, but we're going to have to drop her to get this sewn up." Erica shook her head. "Only Musique could turn a five-minute stitch job into a giant ordeal."

"That's my Musique," Doris said, patting her neck as she walked up to examine the injury. "My, you did do a number on that, didn't you?"

Erica went out to the truck to get more drugs, and I stood by to keep Musique from wandering off. Amelia got Doris caught up on the events, and James drifted over beside me.

"Are you going to lay her down right here in the aisle?" he asked.

"No, we'll have to take her outside to do that," I said. "Concrete is a bad plan all the way around. She'd probably skin her legs up going down, and she'd never get stood up again."

He nodded. "That's what I was thinking, but I didn't know if we could get her to walk now."

He had a good point. Musique was sedated enough to make her a bit wobbly, but she was still ornery enough to fight us off. Walking was going to be a challenge. Fortunately, we only had to go about twenty feet.

"It's going to be a job," I said. "Let's go ahead and start working our way down there."

I tugged on the lead rope, and James got behind her and pushed on her flanks. Musique kept her feet planted until we had overbalanced to the front and she was forced to take a step.

"One down, twenty to go," Doris said with a chuckle. "If she was a little smaller, you could probably just pick her up and carry her out there."

Erica returned with the drugs just as we made the fourth step. It was slow going, but we made steady progress until we got to the door. There was a step down where the concrete stopped, and Musique wasn't interested in negotiating that at all. We pushed and coaxed, but she was firm.

"Okay," Erica said. "Plan C. Let's lift her front leg off the ground, reduce the number of brakes while we're pushing."

She bent down and grabbed the front left foot, and with a bit of cajoling, got it up in the air. "Okay, push!"

I pulled on the rope, and James and Amelia pushed her hind end. Her back legs slid forward on the concrete, and at last she had no choice. She hopped forward, and Erica released her foot at just the right moment. Momentum carried her all the way out the door.

"Yes!" James shouted in triumph. "That was harder than I thought it would be."

"Don't run off celebrating yet," Erica said. "We need to get her a few more steps."

At last, Musique was far enough that she would be safe when we knocked her out. She swayed mildly with her feet spread wide in what is known as the sawhorse position. I grabbed her ear again, which blocked her view as Erica gave her another shot in the neck. We stepped back and chatted for a moment as we waited.

"She's a tough old bird," Doris said. "She's always had a mind of her own, but she was the best hunter pony you could ask for."

"She still has a mind of her own," James said. "She'll walk all the way across the pasture to poop in her stall."

I had to laugh at that. "We used to have that problem with the cats. They'd come inside to use the litterbox, then go back outside."

"How did you solve that?" Amelia asked.

"We got a litter robot," I said. "The cats hate it. Now Oswald is the only cat who will even use the litterbox. Everybody else goes outside. That was the best $400 we ever spent."

"That's solid gold," James agreed.

Musique began squatting, and Erica pulled the lead rope up to the top of her neck to use as a handle. Grabbing it with both hands, Erica shoved hard, and Musique fell back on her haunches. Erica guided her over on her right side, lifting her head to keep it from slamming into the ground. It was a textbook sedation, but it's always easier on a small horse. It's a lot harder to do all that with something that weighs fifteen hundred pounds.

"Showtime," Erica said.

I stuck a towel under the horse's head and draped it across her eyes while Erica ran back in to get the tray. A moment later, she was back. She swapped gloves and got right to work. It was funny how long it took to get to this point, versus how long the actual suturing took. Each stitch drew the flap back in place a bit more, and when she was done, you could hardly tell that anything had happened. It was all over in about five minutes.

"Okay, so how do I take care of this?" Amelia asked.

"Ideally, I'd love for this to get hosed every day or two, but I don't know if you'll be able to get that done with her or not." Erica stripped her gloves off and dropped them in the tray. "What we definitely have to do is keep some triple-antibiotic ointment on it a few times a day. We need to keep it moist. It may get itchy, and if that happens, we can put some hydrocortisone cream on it."

"Is there a special horse ointment, or does the stuff from the drug store work?" James asked. "Because I've got both of those things in the house right now."

"Those will work fine," Erica said. "It doesn't even need to be name brand. Just make sure you get it on there at least twice a day, and three times if you can."

"How long will that take to heal?" Doris asked.

"Oh, probably two weeks," Erica said. "Faces heal really fast."

I gathered up all our stuff and returned it to the truck while we waited for Musique to wake up. I needn't have hurried. It took nearly thirty minutes to get her back on her feet. That's the problem with horses that require a lot of drugs; you have to wait longer for them to wear off. I didn't mind. Hanging out with James is always a good time, and Erica got to catch up with Amelia and Doris.

At last, we returned home. I walked back out in the pasture to the tractor. As I resumed my circles, I thought about Musique being an inside pooper. In a way, that would be better. We'd have more compost to manage, but the pastures wouldn't be dotted with piles. I considered both sides as I dragged the pasture. Thinking about poop, spreading poop, growing grass that will get turned into poop. I'm telling you, my life revolves around poop. I'm not complaining. It sure beats having a poopy life.

Chapter 12

I'm Not Crazy, You're Crazy

I GET TO MEET AN INCREDIBLE VARIETY of people doing what I do. Not unlike paramedics and police, I often meet people at a really bad time for them, which I totally understand. When your horse is trying to maim itself, or your donkey has found a way to break into the feed room and eat a whole bag of grain, you are under a tremendous amount of stress. We all handle that stress in our own way, and I don't expect people to be at their best when I show up at their home with the veterinarian. I wouldn't be at my best in those situations either.

Sometimes, though, we meet people who really raise the eyebrows. I mean really, really raise them, way up high. Sometimes it's the eclectic collection of strange things in their yard.

Sometimes it's the number and variety of animals they have, or their ideas on how they're going to get rich from selling this or that. And sometimes, you meet a person who's just plain nuts.

One day a woman opened the door of the clinic and walked in. She was in her mid-fifties with short red hair and a bright flower-print blouse. She was holding a dog carrier, which she set up on the counter.

"I've got a fox. I think something's wrong with it." She looked around at us, as if waiting for someone to point out that we are an equine veterinary clinic. No one did. Dr. Russel was back in the lab, undoubtedly listening to what was being said up front. Jessica was her tech that day, and she happened to be sitting at the front desk, talking to Amy and me when the woman walked in.

"What's he doing that's strange?" Amy asked, bending down to peer inside the container. Amy used to be the practice manager for a small animal clinic, before she took over our office. She would know better than me if a small animal clinic would see a fox, or if it would need to go someplace like the vet school in Gainesville. People have all kinds of crazy pets and finding the appropriate veterinarian can be a challenge.

"Well, he let us walk up and pet him," the woman said. "That seems kind of weird."

It took a moment for that statement to sink in. The moment that it did was crystal clear, as Jessica slid the chair back against the wall behind her, and Amy backed away to the pharmacy door.

"This isn't your pet, then?" Amy asked.

The woman looked at her like she was crazy. "Pet? Hell no, who has a fox for a pet? This thing just walked up into my yard. My grandkids were playing with it."

In my head, a quarantine list was forming. Dr. Russel came around the corner and said what everyone else was thinking.

"That's probably rabies. Nobody touch it."

The woman looked down the hall as Dr. Russel approached. "Rabies? Are you serious? It didn't bite anyone."

"Everybody out back to the sink, right now. Wash up in chlorhexadine. Justin, help me get the cats locked in the office. They're both in the lab, but we need to decon the counter and the front desk."

A look of dismay crossed the face of the red-haired woman, but she followed Amy and Jessica out the back door to the barn. Dr. Russel and I grabbed the cats and stuck them in Amy's office and closed the door.

Dr. Russel let out a sigh and rubbed her face with her hands. "Oh, my God, what is wrong with people?"

"I know," I said. "What do we do with it? We can't leave it on the front counter."

"Let me get a gown and some gloves on, and I'll put it out front. Can you call animal control? They probably have a process for this."

I pulled out my phone and did a Google search for the local animal control. A man answered on the fourth ring.

"Animal Services."

"Hi, this is Justin Long with Springhill Equine Veterinary Clinic, and we have a fox in a pet carrier with probable rabies. Can you help us out?"

"What are the symptoms?"

"Well, the lady that brought it in was able to pick it up after her grandkids were petting it, and she put it in a dog carrier."

"Okay. We need a list of everyone who has handled the animal. I'll get a truck out there to pick it up. It needs to be isolated from further contact, and all possible areas of bodily fluid exposure must be decontaminated."

"Got it. We're already working on that. I'll get the list for you." I hung up the phone and went to find the others.

It took an hour to get the clinic scrubbed, as we had to hit everything from the doorknobs and floor to the counter and desk, to include the keyboard on the computer. It was a group project. Amy got a list of names, ages, and contact information from the lady of everyone she had seen around the fox. We also gave her some supplies to decon her car. Now that she realized the true danger, she was as paranoid as the rest of us.

It took four days for us to get a call from the state lab, during which time Jessica and Amy were stressed out of their minds, sure that they had been infected. Every time one of them coughed, or felt a twinge of a headache, a new wave of hysteria would ensue. When the call came in, we were all relieved to learn that the fox did not test positive for rabies. It undoubtedly had something bad, but at least it wasn't something that could jump to humans. Everyone rested easier after that news.

That's one kind of crazy, which isn't really crazy, it's just a lack of knowledge and failure to really think about things. There's another kind of crazy, and it's the legitimate kind of crazy. One night, Erica and I got to see some of that firsthand.

We were cleaning the kitchen after supper, when the phone rang.

"Hello, Dr. Lacher." She put the phone on speaker while she added soap to the dishwasher and started it. I was wiping down the table.

"Hi. My name is Crystal, and I've got a problem. One of my mom's goats is sick, and I'm pretty sure it has rabies. I've been calling people all afternoon, but no one can get out here to check it out."

"Where are you located?"

"Micanopy."

I was extremely grateful we had already finished supper. Micanopy is a 45-minute drive, maybe more, depending on where they lived.

"Alright. Tell me about the goat. What's it doing?"

The woman sighed. "It's just laying there, all stiff. It's barely breathing. I know it's going to die, but I'm worried the other goats will get infected. My mom doesn't think it's rabies. She's got dementia, and she's not all there. You've got to help me convince her to get the goat off the property. She just wants to bury it in the yard."

"Alright, it sounds like we definitely need to come out," Erica said, taking the phone off speaker as she grabbed a pen and paper. "It's going to cost somewhere around $450 for us to come see it. Let me get an address from you."

She wrote down the address and motioned me out the door as she explained to the woman how to find the new client form on our website. A minute later we were headed down the driveway. Since we had a long drive in front of us, we listened to a podcast. It's one of our favorite things to do on a car ride.

The road that we found ourselves on was lined with big, expensive houses. They were spread apart, with huge manicured lawns and ornate gates.

"Well, they live in a pretty nice neighborhood," I said. "What's the house number?"

Erica consulted the GPS. "27815. It says it's a mile and a half away yet."

We went around a curve, and the nice neighborhood ended. The sun was setting, turning the sky behind us shades of pink. We passed a swampy area, and the sky was reflected in the water beneath the trees. A mailbox appeared in the deepening dusk, but it wasn't the right number. I slowed down. We passed another mailbox, but it had no number on it. The next mailbox was 28888.

"We passed it," I said, pulling in and turning around. "It had to be the one without a number."

"There weren't any others," Erica agreed. "That has to be it."

We turned into the driveway at the unnumbered mailbox. The dirt drive vanished around a curve in the trees, tall grass growing in the center strip and along the edges. I was nervous about running over something, as it was hard to see anything. I switched the headlights to bright, and as the road straightened out, we found ourselves in what I first thought was a junkyard.

There were giant piles of mysterious things everywhere. Most of them were covered with tattered tarps, and the ground around them was littered in flakes of blue plastic from the deteriorating material. Here and there, old cars sat in twos and threes, with bushes growing out of the engine compartments. A huge department store shelf sat beside one of the cars, loaded with hundreds of jars that twinkled as the headlights passed over them.

"Oh my God," Erica whispered.

"Yeah." I patted her hand. "Don't think about the fact that no one knows where we are. It'll just make it worse."

In front of us was a barely recognizable singlewide trailer. It had so many additions built on out of various materials that it didn't even have a shape. A fallen tree lay across one end of the trailer, with splintered lumber and sheet metal poking up around it. The lighted windows gave it away as a home, or I might have thought it long abandoned. I stopped the vet truck in an open space beside a car that looked like it might actually run. At least the license plate was current.

I took a screenshot of the GPS and sent it out on the clinic

GroupMe with a short message. *In case no one ever sees us again, this is where we are.* I hoped that I had enough signal for it to go out.

As we climbed out of the truck, the car door beside us opened, and a thin blonde woman in her thirties got out.

"Let me get my mom," she said. She leaned back in the car and honked the horn, a long, piercing blast. A moment later the trailer door banged open and a figure appeared on the porch.

"What the hell are you honking about, Trish?" a woman's voice shouted.

"The vet's here for the damn goat," the thin blonde woman shouted back. She turned to us. "She's crazy. Don't listen to her. I spend all my time trying to deal with all her problems. I got my own problems. I just got out of the hospital. I got married a few weeks ago. I don't have time to deal with all her stuff."

Erica and I glanced at one another with a knowing look. We talk about things like this all the time. Young people think they want to be veterinarians because they love animals more than people, but the truth is, being a veterinarian is mostly dealing with people. Sometimes that's easy, and sometimes it isn't. This was shaping up to be one of the kinds that isn't. I swatted at the swarm of mosquitos that was forming around my head, and tried not to think about how many of them were probably carrying encephalitis. This area is a known hotbed of infected mosquitos, and we've seen more than a few unvaccinated horses die from it down here.

"Well, hopefully we can solve one of the problems for you, anyway," Erica said with a smile.

"I didn't get the form filled out," Trish said, as her mother made her way across the yard. "My phone didn't have enough signal."

"Okay, no worries," Erica said, ducking back into the truck. She waved a mosquito away and produced a clipboard and a pen. "You can fill out the paper form. Technology is nice, but it doesn't always work for us."

The mother walked into the glow of the headlights. She had long gray hair hanging down past her shoulders, and bright eyes that sparkled in the glare of the headlights. She was tall, nearly as tall as me, and at 6'2", I don't get to say that very often. Erica smiled and introduced herself.

"Hi, I'm Dr. Lacher. I hear you've got a sick goat."

"I'm sorry my daughter made you come all the way out here," she said, motioning to the back yard. She pulled a small flashlight out of her jacket pocket. "I'll show you where she is, since you're here. I'm Esther, by the way."

We followed her around a table covered in coffee cans, which were filled with rusty bolts and screws. Her daughter stayed at the car, filling out the new client form in the headlights.

"My daughter thinks the goat's got rabies," she said. "You can't listen to her. She's crazy, and she just got out of the mental hospital a few days ago. She doesn't even know what rabies looks like. I've been raising goats for fifty years. I reckon I know if a goat's got rabies."

Erica and I shared another glance as we shuffled between two sheds in a thin trail. The mother sounded like she was as sane as any of us, other than the fact that she was throwing her daughter under the bus in front of strangers. On the back side of the sheds, a row of low pens appeared on the left. More cars and piles of junk went on as far as I could see in every direction. I officially had a Class A case of the willies.

"Wanda's in the first pen," Esther said, shining her

flashlight over the gate.

Erica turned on her headlamp, which lit up the area like daylight. We stepped around the hulk of an old riding mower and stopped beside the pen. Inside, a big tan and white goat lay on its side. Her legs were locked out rigid, in the position we call "The Sawhorse". This is never a good sign, regardless of what kind of animal it is.

Erica slipped on a pair of rubber gloves and tried to open the gate. The poop and bedding on the inside wouldn't let the gate go in, and the tall weeds on the outside didn't want to let it pull out. She gave it a hard tug, and it opened enough for her to slip in.

"Hey, Wanda," she murmured, squatting down. "Easy now, I'm just going to take your temperature." Wanda couldn't move if she wanted to, and I wasn't even sure if she knew we were there. Her breathing was fast and shallow, and her eyes were vacant. Erica slipped the rectal thermometer in place and put her stethoscope on to listen to Wanda's vitals as she waited for the thermometer to beep.

The goat in the next pen came over to the wall. The pens were built with an assortment of hog wire, pallets, and scraps of chain link fencing, and the piece that separated the first two pens was mostly pallet. A black nose poked through a gap between the boards for a moment, then disappeared as a yellow eye came into view.

"Well, the neighbor goat seems to be feeling pretty good," I said. "Have you had any trouble with any of the other animals, or is it just Wanda?"

"Everybody else is fine," Esther said. "If there was something with rabies running around here, it would've got the chickens before it got the goats. My daughter's crazy. She's in and out of the mental hospital all the time. She thinks she knows everything. I've been raising goats for fifty years. I reckon I'd know if Wanda had rabies."

"When were they last vaccinated and dewormed?" Erica asked.

Esther scratched her arm as she thought. "Well, I think it was last year. Maybe the year before. It ain't been very long, anyway. Let's see, Kenny gave them a shot for me when I had surgery. I guess it was four or five years ago. They last a while."

"Um, probably not that long." Erica stood up. "I don't think it's rabies, but I can't rule it out. She presents more like a Tetanus case. Either way, we need to euthanize her. She's in bad shape."

Esther shook her head. "I knew it wasn't rabies. I've had goats for fifty years."

"We need to euthanize her," Erica said again. "I need your permission to put her to sleep."

"Oh, sure, I know she's going. Go ahead."

Erica wiped a mosquito off her cheek with her shoulder. "Justin, can you run back to the truck and grab 30 ccs of euth and the clippers?"

"Got it." I took off back to the truck. It was almost full dark now, and I used the light on my phone to find my way back to the vet truck through the maze of junk. Mosquitos swarmed me, and by the time I opened the rear hatch, I was pretty sure I had encephalitis. Trish walked around the corner of the truck as I was pulling up the drugs and handed me the clipboard.

"I got everything filled out," she said. "Are you going to kill the goat?"

I nodded, as I double-checked that I had the right amount of euthanasia solution in the syringe. "Yes, she's in bad shape."

Trish clutched my arm and whispered with intensity. "You

have to tell my mom that Kenny is going to bury the goat at his house, and you're going to drop it off. Otherwise she'll want to bury it here, and we can't do that. It's got rabies."

"Who's Kenny?" I asked, carefully capping the needle before she accidently caused me to stab one of us with euthanasia solution.

"He's her nephew. He helps her out when I'm out of town. But you got to send the goat's head off to get rabies tested, and she'll never go for it, 'cause she don't think it's got rabies. I'm afraid she's going to end up with rabies."

I reached over to get the clippers out of the bottom drawer, and she let go of my arm. "Okay. Let me get us through this part, and we'll work that out afterwards." I put on a pair of gloves, just to be on the safe side. I didn't know what the goat had, but it looked like I'd be carrying it out of there, and I was already emotionally maxed out on high-risk virus exposure for the day. There was a roll of large black trash bags beside the printer, and I grabbed a couple of them and stuffed them in my back pocket. Every bit of added protection helps, right?

"She's got dementia," Trish said, following me back to the goat pen. "She doesn't know what's going on half the time. She's crazy, but she don't think she's crazy."

I swatted a mosquito on my neck, unsure whether I was more uncomfortable from the possibility of getting encephalitis, or from dealing with two somewhat unhinged people. It was a tough call. Trish continued to explain how crazy her mother was until we reached the pen. I handed the clippers and the syringe to Erica, grateful for the moment of silence.

Erica clipped a square on Wanda's neck and handed me the clippers. Next, she clamped her thumb across the square, and a vein popped up. She whispered something to Wanda, patted her on the head, and slid the needle in. It was all over in a second. Erica capped the needle and handed it to me.

"They're gonna drop her off at Kenny's," Trish announced. "I called him, and he wants to bury her over there. He said he'll put her out under the tree, with the cat."

I saw Erica's eyebrow twitch, but she didn't say anything. Being in the middle of this was so awkward for me already, the last thing I wanted was to have to lie to one of them on behalf of the other one. It was a tough spot. Trish was technically the client in this situation, as she was the one who called us, and the one paying for everything. I hoped that Esther wouldn't challenge her on this.

"Well, the vet said it's probably Tetanus," Esther said. "I don't know why he wants to bury it there. He must be drunk."

"Probably so. The vet said they'd take her over there." Trish looked at me out of the corner of her eye.

"We'll take care of her," I said. I slipped into the pen with Erica and pulled the trash bags out of my back pocket. "We'll have to bag her up, and then we'll take her over there."

Erica did a final vitals check to confirm everything, and we carefully put the first bag around her feet and worked it up her torso. Esther and Trish watched in silence. It was hard to tell what they were feeling. We slid the second bag over the first, starting at the head this time. Her legs were poking straight out, and we tried hard not to rip the bag on her hooves. When it was done, I stood up and handed the syringe and the clippers back to Erica.

"I'll grab her if you'll carry this stuff," I said. She nodded.

Wanda was surprisingly light for her size. I was expecting her to be borderline unmanageable, but once I had her cradled in my arms, carrying her to the truck wasn't bad, except for the mosquitos buzzing around my ears and eyes. Not being able to swat them away was annoying. Erica walked behind me, and the light from her headlamp lit the path for me. We slid Wanda into the folded-down back seat of the vet truck.

"Okay," Erica said, picking up the clipboard from the bumper where I had left it. "Give me just a minute to get this put in the computer, and we'll be all set."

"Go on to the house, mom," Trish said. "I'll be there in a minute."

"Sorry you had to come out," Esther said, turning to the trailer. "I've had goats for fifty years. I knew she didn't have rabies." She shuffled off into the darkness.

"See?" Trish said. "She's crazy." She shook her head. "I called five other vets today, and nobody would come. They probably have her on a list of crazy people."

I chuckled, unsure of the appropriate way to respond. "I'm sorry it was so hard to get some help. Next time, call us first."

"Oh, I will."

Erica printed off the bill, handed it to Trish and returned her credit card. "Okay, you're all set. I recommend vaccinating all the goats immediately and getting them on a regular annual schedule. As soon as I get rabies results from the state lab, I'll let you know. Is this a good number to reach you?" She pointed to the new client form.

"Yep, that's my cell." Trish turned and walked towards the house without another word.

Erica and I looked at each other, shrugged, and climbed in the truck. A socially awkward moment was a much better conclusion to this visit than a lot of other things that might have happened. We remained silent until we got turned around and out of the driveway. Once we were on the pavement, I let out a huge sigh.

"Oh, my God," I said.

We looked at each other and burst into gales of laughter.

"Was that not the most insane thing that's ever happened?" she asked.

"You should have heard the daughter grilling me back at the truck."

"You should have heard the mom while you were gone!"

"They both need to spend about five days a week with a therapist."

"I don't know which one was crazier."

"Me, either."

"Did she say she got married recently?"

"I think so."

"Just... Wow."

We rode in silence for a few minutes, trying to find some sort of equalization.

"Do you think the goat has rabies?" I asked.

"No, it's definitely not a rabies case."

"What are we going to do with it?"

Erica sighed. "Well, she wants it tested, and I charged her for it, so we're going to send it off. Do you mind taking the body to the crematorium tomorrow?"

"Huh. I'd rather drop it off at Kenny's house."

We laughed again, reveling in the emotional release.

"I think I got encephalitis while we were there," I said.

"Oh, me too. Without a doubt."

It was late when we dropped Wanda off at the clinic and finally got home. A long hot shower had never felt so good, and I slept like a rock.

A few days later we got confirmation from the state lab: it wasn't rabies. Erica called and left a message for Trish, but we never heard back from her.

Sometimes finding your way through an emergency is complicated due to the people, not the animal. Had the goats been properly vaccinated, none of this would have happened. Had a vet been involved as soon as the goat started showing signs, it might have lived. It's hard to say. Wanda was a victim, though, and that's the part that I struggle with. Then again, Esther and Trish were both struggling with their own challenges and were victims in their own way. In the real world, it gets complicated. The important thing is to try to do what's best for both the animal and the people, and find whatever balance you can, and I think we did the best we could have done with that.

Chapter 13

A PAIN IN THE NECK

SOMETIMES WE SEE HORSES with injuries that should have been treated days before they got to us. It's easy to rush to judgement on people in these situations and blame them for not being better horse owners. Sometimes that's a justifiable attitude, even if it's not necessarily the most appropriate. Other times the full story comes out, and you realize that the exact same thing could happen to you and your horse, and you couldn't have prevented it any more than they did. I've seen enough of those now to give people the benefit of the doubt.

I happened to be at the clinic one morning replacing a water spigot that got knocked off the wall. Water spigots are one of those things you see every day, use constantly, and never think about until something happens. Earlier that morning, something happened. We were moving a table in the aisle, and the table leg hit the spigot and broke it off. Instantly, a jet of water shot across the aisle and blasted the opposite wall.

I raced out to the well to shut off the valve to the building. The well is inside our storage shed, and buried beneath everything, as we've never needed to access it for anything. I threw boxes and signs out of the way, buckets and feed pans, and finally got to the main valve. The aisle in the clinic was steadily getting flooded out, mind you, and nothing ever happens the easy way when you're in a rush.

I grabbed the handle and twisted, but it didn't budge. Apparently, I was the first person to ever try to shut off the valve since it got installed, and it didn't want to move. I tried with both hands, straining with all my might. Nothing. Sometimes sudden movements work better to free up seized things, so I tried jerking the handle. I was getting frustrated, and my decision-making abilities were rapidly decreasing. With a final surge of rage, I grabbed the handle and gave it everything I had. It broke off in my hand, and I threw it out the door in disgust.

There was only one other way to stop the fire hydrant-like spray in the aisle. I ran back into the clinic and opened the breaker box, praying that everything was properly labeled. There, at the bottom, was the breaker I was looking for: WELL. I flipped it to the off position and ran back out to the aisle.

While the techs used the squeegee and the leaf blower to clear the water out of the building, I ran to the hardware store and got some replacement parts. I had never replaced a spigot before, but there was enough pipe sticking out of the wall that I felt confident about getting it done myself. I'm starting to realize that this is how you become a jack of all trades. The older you get, the more things go wrong, and you just have to figure it out. I wish someone had told me that when I was twenty. I grew up thinking that everyone knew how to do everything, except me. Ah, well, such is life.

I got the new spigot installed, and they got the floor dry. Not five minutes later, a call came into the clinic: someone was hauling in an emergency. By this point, I couldn't even remember what I had started out to do before the water spigot fiasco, so I decided to wait and see what was coming in case they needed help. We didn't have to wait long.

An old F-350 dually came through the gate pulling a stock trailer. The truck was probably black under the coating of grime, and I knew they had the same problem we had at our house. When you live near a lime rock quarry, you can tell at a glance when others do, too. It's a curse when you have a dark vehicle, because the lime rock dust builds up on the road, and when it rains, it ends up covering your vehicle like a white paste.

A stocky woman jumped out of the driver's seat and quickly walked to the back of the trailer. Her daughter ran down the other side, and we walked out to greet them as they opened the trailer door.

"Hi, I'm Dr. Allison. What have we got here?"

The woman clucked at the horse and quickly shook hands with Dr. Allison. "Hi, I'm Helen, and this is Squirrel. I think she's got an infection in her neck."

A gray horse backed off the trailer. She had a huge angry red welt on the right side of her neck, with a yellow crust on it.

"Oh, no," Dr. Allison said. "What did you do?"

Cassie, the technician, took the lead rope and walked Squirrel towards the stocks in the aisle as Helen explained.

"I've been gone for two weeks, and my mom was taking

care of the horses for me. When I got home this morning, she told me Squirrel had run into a tree branch and got a splinter last week, but she pulled it out, and everything was fine." She gestured at the horse. "Obviously everything is not fine."

I followed them into the aisle, grateful that I'd finished the spigot replacement before they got here. Once Squirrel was in the stocks, Dr. Allison began her examination. She ran her hands around Squirrel's neck, then stood in front of her and felt both sides at the same time. I stood back with Helen and watched as the crusty bit came off in Dr. Allison's hand. She probed the wound, which did not look like it was healing much, especially if it was a week old.

"Alright, let's clean this up," Dr. Allison said. "Cassie, I need the ultrasound. My guess is that there's still something in there, and the body's having a hard time pushing it out. We've got a pretty good infection going here, too."

She began cleaning the gunk and funk away from the edges of the wound. It looked like Squirrel had been rolling in the dirt, as horses do, and the dirt had stuck to the open wound. It probably looked worse than it was, since the horse was light gray.

Cassie had the ultrasound machine set up by the time the wound was cleaned, and Dr. Allison began scanning the lumpy area. Most people are familiar with the classic ultrasound image of a pregnant woman with a happy baby curled up in her womb, distinct and clear. I have personally never seen anything on an ultrasound image that was distinct and clear on a horse. Admittedly, a baby is a very recognizable thing, as opposed to an unknown foreign object inside a maze of muscles, tendons, veins, and whatever else is in there. The point is, I couldn't see anything except static on the screen, which is about all I ever see. That's how it is as a horse doctor's husband. No training on things like reading ultrasounds and x-rays.

Dr. Allison got way more out of the ultrasound than I did, of course. She froze the image and pointed to a bit of static on the screen. "It looks like there's definitely something still in there. I can't tell how big it is because it's deeper than the probe can see, but we'll see if we can get it out."

They got the tools ready, and she gave Squirrel a shot on the other side of her neck. "I'm giving her some sedation, and we'll numb the area around the wound. It's probably very tender, and we don't want her to feel this."

When everything was ready, Dr. Allison slid her finger into the wound and felt around. She stuck some clamps in beside her finger and began trying to grab the object, which was presumably the rest of the tree branch that Squirrel had run into. It took several tries, but she finally got the clamps locked on.

It was an awkward situation, and I was glad it wasn't up to me to get it done. She had to get the piece of wood out, but she needed to do so without breaking it, or causing any more damage to the tissue. This was compounded by the way it didn't want to come out. Dr. Allison tugged firmly, wiggling it slightly, but it didn't move. I had flashbacks to the water valve out at the pump.

"It's really in there," she said, resting her hand for a moment. "I'm sure there's all kinds of swelling, and that's making life difficult for us."

Helen shook her head. "I'm gonna kill my mom. She should have called the vet as soon as it happened."

I chuckled. It's always tough when your mom is involved, and something goes wrong.

Dr. Allison reset the clamp at a different angle and tried again. She pulled harder, widening her stance. The clamp slipped off, bringing a shred of wood with it. Blood was oozing out of the wound, making it hard to see what was going on inside and making everything slippery. She stuck the clamp in again, carefully placing it, and began working it side to side, and up and down. Finally, it began to move.

The tip of the splinter came out like a bloody spear. She tugged, working it back and forth, and suddenly it slid out, like a stick coming out of the mud. It came out and out and out, and we all stood there in shock. This was hardly a splinter. It was nearly a foot long. As soon as it was out of Squirrel's neck, pus and infected goo began pouring out the hole like a volcano. The smell was horrendous, but all I could think about was how good it must feel to have that giant tree branch out of her neck.

Dr. Allison began pushing around the edges of the opening, helping the infected goo work its way out. Blood and pus coated Squirrel from her neck all the way down her chest and front leg, and if someone had just walked up and seen her, it would probably look like she was the victim of an axe murderer. The floor, so recently clean, was a mess.

They flushed the wound, trying to get everything out that they could. Squirrel got a horse-sized dose of antibiotics and some pain meds, and a good prognosis of recovery. I was glad to hear that. With a stick that big in her neck, it could have easily gone the other way.

I posted a video of the splinter removal on our YouTube channel. It's not for the faint of heart or weak of stomach, but if you're interested, you can find it. Just search for Springhill Equine on YouTube, and look through our video library.

Squirrel definitely would have been better off with

immediate vet care at the time of the incident, but this is what I was talking about at the beginning, how we don't always have control of what happens. Seeing this situation unfold prompted me to be more direct with people who horse sit for us when we're away from home. We now have a sign in our feed room that says, *Call the vet first, ask questions later!* It's a good rule of thumb. After all, what's more important to us than our animals?

Chapter 14

EXPERT SUPERVISION

CLEANING THE BARN IS A GOOD TASK for a lot of reasons. Scooping poop will help keep your ego from getting too inflated, for starters. It's also a great time to do some thinking, and thinking time is getting harder and harder to come by these days. I do my best thinking in the shower, and my second-best thinking while cleaning stalls. I don't have to do it every day, so that's probably helpful in maintaining the magic. Then again, some people do it every day, and swear by it.

I was scrubbing out water buckets one Saturday evening, while Erica pushed the wheelbarrow out to the compost bin to dump it. We built an aerated composting system since we produce so much horse poop. There are three bins, each of which holds about thirty days' worth of poop and bedding. So, we dump poop in every day for thirty days, then it sits for thirty days with air being pumped through it a few times a day, then it sits for thirty days without the air. After that, we have pretty good compost that we can safely spread on the pastures. With the three bins, we rotate from one to the next every thirty days.

One of the side effects of composting is that you start learning more about how it works, and then you start to get obsessed with managing and tweaking it. That's what happened to Erica, anyway. She loves to check the temperature in the pile, monitor fungus growth, and all that kind of stuff. I've even caught her looking at moisture meters on the internet. Like I said, it can become an obsession.

I finished rinsing out the buckets and started returning them to their stalls and filling them. It's funny how some horses drink tons of water, some horses use their hay to make tea (and a mess), and some horses don't even acknowledge that the water is there. Gigi is one to race over to the water bucket in the pasture as soon as you turn her out, and drink ten gallons of water, as if she didn't have any in her stall. I guess the outside water just tastes better.

I was about to go give Erica a hard time for playing with the compost bin too long, when I heard her phone ring.

"Hello, Dr. Lacher."

I spun around and went to the other end of the barn. The only thing left to do was put out flakes of hay for the next day, and if we were about to go to work, I wanted to be finished with everything before we left.

I grabbed three flakes of timothy and two flakes of alfalfa, sliding the door closed behind me with a foot. Erica came around the corner as I was dropping the last flake in Ernie's stall.

"We've got a colic," she said, leaving the wheelbarrow in the aisle as she pointed to the truck. "I've got to change shoes quick. Do you need anything upstairs?"

I shook my head. "I'm good, although if you want to grab a granola bar, I'd eat it."

A few minutes later, we were headed down the driveway. They were only about fifteen minutes away from us, which seems unusual to me. I have a theory about horses that live nearby never having emergencies. It's not really based on any evidence, it's just something I think about when we have to drive a long way in the middle of the night.

"Who are we going to see?" I asked.

"New client, we haven't seen them before. The horse's name is Rowdy."

We turned off the pavement and onto a dirt road. After a few miles, we turned onto another dirt road, and finally arrived at the address. A white singlewide trailer sat back from the road, with kid's toys scattered about. I recognized some of them, such as the Big Wheel and the Fred Flintstone mobile. Behind the trailer was a big metal shop surrounded by cars. To the left of the shop was a newly fenced paddock. A horse stood inside, and two people were at the gate. I drove around the trees and pulled up next to them, and we hopped out.

"How y'all doing?" I asked.

"Hi, I'm Tara. This is Pete, my boyfriend." She was a short, petite blonde in her late thirties. She stuck her cigarette in her mouth and shook my hand.

Pete leaned against the gate, not offering to participate in the introductions. He wore a camouflage t-shirt and blue jeans and held a can of Budweiser in one hand. Dark hair stuck out from under his camouflage hat, and a three-day stubble covered

174 · JUSTIN B. LONG

his chin. The smirk on his face told me that he thought it was ridiculous that we were here.

I followed Erica to the back of the truck to get what she needed for the exam. Tara came back a moment later.

"I don't know what's wrong with him," she said. "I've only had him a few months. He's the first horse I've had since I was a teenager."

Erica nodded. "Has he been rolling a lot?"

Tara shrugged. "I guess. I mean, he's been up and down all afternoon. Pete don't think we need a vet, though."

I noticed Erica's jaw clench ever so slightly. "Has he had any medication? Did you give him Banamine or anything?"

"No medicine," Tara said. She shuffled her feet and looked down. "Pete said Rowdy was just constipated. He put some mineral oil in the water hose and ran that into his, you know, into his butt. I don't know if that helped any."

Erica paused, and turned to look at Tara. "He put a water hose inside the horse and ran it?"

Tara nodded, looking uncomfortable. Pete stood up from the gate and wandered over. "That's how we always done it," he said, taking a pull off the beer can. "You don't need no vet for that."

Erica glanced at Pete, then turned back to Tara. "That's extremely dangerous. The tissue inside there is delicate, and if it gets torn, you can kill the horse. It's also pointless. If everything went perfect, you might get the water and mineral oil five feet into his small colon, but impactions are usually twenty-five to fifty feet inside there, maybe as much as seventy-five feet. That's assuming that it really is an impaction, and not something else. The next problem is that the water is going the wrong way. You have to go in from the other end to get it flushed out this end."

Pete snorted and shook his head. "It worked every time I ever did it. Two or three times. Leave it to a woman to call a damn vet."

I cringed internally, but Erica ignored him and handed me the tray. "Let's go take a look at him."

Tara led us through the gate and over to Rowdy, grabbing a halter off the fence post as she went by. Rowdy was standing stretched out, looking back at his left side every few seconds. Water and mineral oil coated the backs of his legs and his tail. I sat the tray down and took the halter from Tara and slipped it over his head.

"Hey, buddy," I said, scratching his ears. "We're going to get you fixed up."

Erica put the stethoscope on and began working her way around him, listening to his heartbeat and gut sounds. As she walked behind him, she shook her head in disgust. "Your poor tail is a wreck," she said. A minute later, she pulled the stethoscope out of her ears and set it in the tray.

"His heart rate is low, so that's good," she said, pulling on a palpation sleeve, which is a plastic glove that goes all the way to her armpit. "He doesn't have a lot of gut sounds, but I have no idea how much water got pumped into him, and that could certainly impact things. I'm going to try to palpate him and see what's going on in there."

She lubed up the glove and stuck her hand inside his rectum. I watched her feel around slowly, and it took me a moment to realize she was trying to see if the end of the hose had torn him anywhere. Satisfied, she moved her arm in all the way to the shoulder. Within seconds, her scrub top was coated in mineral oil from Rowdy's rear end and tail. She had to be seething inside, but she did a good job keeping her outward appearance calm. I held his head while she palpated him, but he was very well-behaved and didn't move.

"He's pretty gassed up," she said, shifting her position to get a different angle. A few seconds later she withdrew her arm and pulled the sleeve off. "Despite what Pete says, you do need a veterinarian, and you did the right thing by calling. Rowdy's going to get a smooth-muscle relaxer, which is a drug that will help his intestines relax so he can pass the gas. We're also going to pump some water with electrolytes into him to help him rehydrate and get everything moving normally again."

Tara nodded, glancing sideways at the gate where Pete was lounging. "Whatever you think is best. His buddy has horses, and he said he knows how to doctor them. I didn't know what to do."

"If you have a horse, you should have a veterinarian," I said. "It's always a good plan."

Erica drew up a syringe and gave Rowdy a shot. "That's a pain med, which will make him feel better. We're going to run to the truck and get the pump bucket and the other drugs, and we'll be right back."

Pete swallowed the rest of his beer, tossed the can on the ground, and looked away as we passed him at the gate. I couldn't decide if he was embarrassed or indignant. I understand the subculture that exists that doesn't believe in using veterinarians, as I grew up in it. It's not even that they don't believe in veterinarians, it's that they don't believe in spending money on anything like that. For my dad, the idea of paying someone else to do something for him, whether it was a mechanic or a plumber or an electrician, was akin to the idea of cutting off his leg. I'm glad I managed to escape that mindset. My time is far too valuable to me to do everything myself, just to save a buck.

Also, there can be victims to that mindset, like Rowdy. We see it all the time with horses that don't get vaccinated, or don't get dental care, or get home treatments for life-threatening conditions. It's just sad.

Erica is far too professional to ever say anything in front of someone, but once we got to the back of the truck, she gave me a long look that said plenty. Nothing makes her mad like an arrogant man with a chauvinistic attitude, except perhaps an arrogant idiot with a chauvinistic attitude. This is another thing we see on a regular basis. There are a lot of men (and, sadly, sometimes women) that insist on talking to me, rather than to her, despite the fact that she's the doctor, and I'm just there to hold the horse and carry the heavy stuff. These are usually the guys that refuse to call her 'Dr. Lacher,' and instead refer to her as 'Miss Erica' or something similar. I just smile when this happens, because it's going to cost them an extra fifty dollars for being a jerk.

I took the bucket over to the water hose to fill it and bent down to grab it. My hand was nearly on the hose when I realized it was covered in mineral oil and slimy poop. Pete's home remedy just kept on causing problems. I changed plans and went over to the water trough and filled it there. Erica met me at the horse.

Rowdy didn't like the tube going up his nose, but no one ever does. I have a ton of empathy for them in this situation. While I've never had a tube up my nose, I have a great imagination, and I can feel the itchy, tickling, maddening sensation all the way through my sinuses every time we do this. He calmed down after a minute, and Erica made a show of checking the tube.

"You can wind up with the tube in the lungs if you aren't

careful," she said to Tara. "That would drown him, so don't ever let anyone do this that isn't a veterinarian."

I just managed to stop the grin that was spreading across my face, and started pumping water and electrolytes into Rowdy. Now that the tube was in place and the drugs were kicking in, he stood quietly and let it happen. When we were done, I took everything back to the truck. Normally, I clean the tube and the bucket out on the spot, but I knew what the hose looked like, and decided I'd wait until we got home to do that part.

Pete had wandered off, and Tara took the opportunity to start asking questions. I desperately wanted to give her some relationship advice, but that would have been wildly inappropriate, so I kept my part of the conversation to the topic of horses.

"What kind of advice do you have for new horse owners?" she asked. Erica was typing up the aftercare instructions, so I fielded this one.

"At a minimum, you need to get him vaccinated twice a year with the core vaccines," I said. "Even if he never goes anywhere, mosquitoes can bring in encephalitis, West Nile, and things like that. He also needs to have his teeth floated every year by a veterinarian."

"How about feed?"

"What are you feeding now?" I asked.

"Sweet feed, and he's got a round roll of hay."

I closed the hatchback. "He'd be better off eating grain. Sweet feed doesn't have much nutritional value. You'll also find that it's probably cheaper to feed him the expensive feed, because he won't need near as much at a time. How many scoops do you give him?"

"Three in the morning, and three at night."

"Yeah, if you give him a senior diet, he'll only need like half a scoop twice a day. It costs more per bag, but you don't feed near as much, and you don't have to give him any supplements. I'd also give him a flake of alfalfa or peanut every day. That will reduce the colic risk from the coastal hay."

I could tell she was struggling with that. It's hard to convince people to spend twenty dollars for a bag of feed when they're currently spending seven or eight. I doubted that she would have much luck selling Pete on the idea, anyway.

"Anything else?" she asked. "I'm trying to get things set up for him here. We just got the fence done a few weeks ago."

I debated about what to say regarding the fence but decided to be honest for Rowdy's sake. "I would get rid of the barbed wire. We sew up horses all the time that slice themselves open on it."

"Really?" A look of surprise spread across her face. "Pete said it was the only fence that would keep him in."

"Electricity is your friend," I said with a smile. "You've got good no-climb fencing there, and that's perfect. Just replace that strand of barbed wire on top with an electric wire, and you won't have any laceration problems."

A small blue car pulled into the driveway and parked nearby. A young woman got out and grabbed a toddler out of the back seat.

"Hey, mom, what's up?" she asked.

"Rowdy was still colicking. I had to call the vet." She glanced around. "Probably should have called the vet to start with," she muttered, taking a deep drag on her cigarette.

Erica stepped around the truck and handed Tara some papers. "Okay, this one has his care plan written out, so you don't have to remember all this stuff. We're going to let him hang out for a while so the drugs can do their thing. In an hour or so, I want to offer him a bite of food, something just to see if he's interested in eating. If he has an appetite, then that's a good sign, that's what we're looking for. We're going to go light on breakfast in the morning, and then tomorrow night we can go back to a regular diet. I heard you guys talking about feed, and I definitely recommend adding the daily flake of alfalfa or peanut hay to his diet. If he's not interested in food in an hour, I want you to call me. It doesn't mean we're coming back out, but I might talk you through some other options, okay?"

"Yeah, okay," Tara said, glancing over her shoulder. "Look, I really appreciate you giving me all this information. It's hard to learn all this stuff, you know?"

"Learning about horses is a full-time job," Erica said with a smile. "Here's your credit card back, and here's our business card. You should check out our website. We've got a great blog with tons of free information about horse care."

Tara nodded. "I will, thanks."

We pulled out of the yard and onto the dirt road. Erica didn't say anything for a while. When we got to the asphalt, I broke the silence.

"Looks like your scrub top is probably ruined."

She looked down. "Yeah, we'll never get the mineral oil out of this. My pants are probably shot, too."

"Did you charge them extra for the clothes?" I asked with a chuckle.

Erica let out a sigh. "It's tough. That guy was an asshole, but it's not like he's paying the bill."

"Right," I agreed. "Punishing her for making bad relationship decisions isn't going to teach him anything."

"He's lucky he didn't kill that horse," she said. "What a piece of work."

We rode the rest of the way home in silence. Sometimes making the world a better place for horses is hard. For horses like Rowdy, the deck is stacked against them. If Pete had anything to do with it, Rowdy would never eat a decent meal, or get a vaccine or a dental float, and Pete's ignorance would cut Rowdy's life expectancy in half. That's not fair to Rowdy, but we only have so much influence. I hoped that what I told Tara would be enough to make a difference. I guess time will tell.

Chapter 15

You Ate What?

I WAS SITTING AT MY DESK ONE MORNING, intermittently watching Gerald and the rental sheep eating my mother-in-law's flower garden, while I edited a manuscript. The sheep require almost no maintenance from us, but an inordinate amount of my time still goes into watching them. They like to stand on her porch and munch on leaves. Sometimes one of the dogs will come out the dog door unexpectedly, which causes a great deal of surprise to both the sheep and the dogs, and that's always fun to see. I'm convinced that one of these days, Gerald is going to get brave and go through the dog door into the house, and I don't want to miss it when that happens. We're talking about top-shelf entertainment, here!

The sheep wandered away from the house, so it didn't look like it was going to happen this time. I went back to my book, determined to get at least one more chapter edited before heading to the clinic. A moment later, my phone dinged, letting me know there was a message on GroupMe. It was Dr. Russel.

Choke coming in. Can we get a stall ready?

That was rather unusual. Choking horses generally clear themselves out within a half hour or so. They can still breathe despite being choked, so it isn't life-threatening. For the horses that don't clear their own choke, it's usually just a matter of giving them a smooth-muscle relaxer and tubing them with a few gallons of water to clear it. They almost always choke on feed, as opposed to grass or hay, and the water dissolves it into mush. It makes a mess, but it's rarely a big deal. This one must be an exceptional choke.

I muted the phone and buckled down for a solid half hour of productivity with no more distractions. Editing is much less fun than writing, at least for me, and I had to be tough with myself to avoid distractions. That meant no Facebook, no email, no sheep, and no dogs. Sometimes it's hard to be a writer.

When I arrived at the clinic to get the bank deposit and the recycling, the choking horse was already there. Jessica, one of our technicians, was carrying the scope out to the barn. That piqued my curiosity, and I followed her out the door.

Dr. Russel was in the stall with the horse. He was a paint with a white face and blue eyes, and at the moment, he had an NG tube going up his nose. She worked the tube in a circle as Stacey, the other tech, slowly pumped water into it. Water poured back out of his nostrils and pooled on the floor of the stall.

"Okay, that's enough," Dr. Russel said. "Let's get the scope in here and see what's going on." She carefully pulled the tube out of the horse's nose, and Stacey moved the pump and bucket out of the way.

Jessica had the scope out of the case and was turning on the tablet. We hadn't had this new scope very long, and I was excited to see it in action. Our previous scope was the old-fashioned kind that you had to look through like a telescope. I won't mention any names, but someone accidently stepped on the tip of that scope and broke the camera. Okay, it was me. I broke the old scope. Anyway, now we have this new one, and it sends the image to a tablet screen so everyone can see what's going on. It takes pictures, records video, and all kinds of neat stuff.

"Okay," Jessica said, carrying the scope into the stall. "We need someone to hold the tablet, and we need someone to keep Justin from stepping on the scope."

I laughed with them. "Yeah, yeah, rub it in. I'm happy to hold the tablet." I grabbed it off the table and followed her into the stall. "What's this guy's name?"

"Bob." Stacey rolled her eyes.

I chuckled. It always strikes me as funny when people name an animal Bob, whether it's a cat, dog, horse or donkey. If we ever get a goose, his name is going to be Bob. Don't worry, with Erica's aversion to geese, it's never going to happen.

"Does someone have the lube in their pocket?" Dr. Russel asked.

"Right here." Stacey produced the tube of lubricant, and Dr. Russel squirted some on the tip of the scope and worked it around the shaft. It was a three-meter scope, and a bit big for this sort of application, but it was all we had. Dr. Russel draped the dry end around her neck, and Jessica helped her keep it off the ground as she prepared to insert it in the horse's nostril.

I positioned myself across from Dr. Russel so that she could see the screen as she managed the scope. Stacey held the horse's halter, and Jessica stood at the end of the scope, ready to steer it as necessary and manage the controls. My job would be to hold the screen, and take pictures and video as directed. Having done this before, I knew that my tendency was to unconsciously tilt the screen up to where I could see it, thus spoiling the view for the doctor, who is the one that actually needs to see it. I reminded myself to keep that in mind this time.

If you're not familiar with these endoscopes, they're pretty amazing. It's a ten-foot long black snake, essentially. They're about as big around as your finger, with a control box on the end. From the control box, you can turn the tip left and right, and up and down. You can also insert a syringe into a fitting and pump air or water through the scope. This will clear fluids and other debris off the tip of the camera to keep your field of vision clear. They also do things like take tissue samples, fluid samples, and probably some other things I don't know about.

"Okay, which way is up?" Jessica asked. They peered at the screen as Dr. Russel held the end of the scope out in front of her. I looked down at the screen and saw a sideways image of myself.

"Okay, we need to turn it counter-clockwise," Dr. Russel said. They rotated the scope until the image was the right way up. Having asked about this before, I can tell you that it's important to do this so that when they try to angle the tip to the left to see something, it turns the right way. You can do it without having it aligned, but there's a lot more fumbling around.

With the camera aligned, she stuck the tip in Bob's nose. The tiny ring of LED lights around the camera put out an incredible amount of light. The screen showed a wet pink tunnel. Some of the tissue was red, which was probably irritation from being tubed twice already. I focused on keeping the screen pointed at Dr. Russel, but bent over so I could see it, too.

It was like watching a weird roller coaster video, or maybe a weird water park ride. The camera slowly slid forward. The black tunnel vanished over a drop off ahead, which meant we were already closing in on his neck. The anticipation of the unknown was ramping up. I was dying to know what was in his throat, keeping him from being able to swallow. It was tough enough to resist the tube and the water, and I had visions of all kinds of crazy things that he might have swallowed. It could be an Easter egg, or a drain stopper, or a piece of plastic, anything. The possibilities were endless.

Dr. Russel interrupted my daydreaming. "Justin, I can't see the screen."

Somehow the tablet was facing up instead of forward. I blushed, flipping the screen back down. "My bad."

They all giggled at me. The camera crept forward, finally reaching the downturn.

"Point it up just a bit," Dr. Russel murmured. "We want to make sure we go into the esophagus, and not the trachea."

She pushed it forward, and the view angled down. I could see where the airway split off from the trachea as the camera went by. The wet walls glistened in the bright light. As the esophagus straightened out, Jessica brought the aim of the scope back to center. There, directly below the camera, was our obstruction. We all had the same thought at the same time.

"That looks like shavings," Dr. Russel said. She slid the scope in a little further. "Justin, can you take a picture of that, please?"

Indeed, the mass in the middle of Bob's throat looked just like the floor of the stall we were standing in. I tapped the screen, and it saved the image. I did it again a few more times, as they don't always come out clear, and it's hard to go back and take another one.

"What do we do about that?" Stacey asked. "If the tube and the water didn't push through it, what else can you do?"

Dr. Russel shrugged. "I don't know. I've never seen a horse eat enough bedding to choke himself before."

"We need a shop vac with a tiny hose," I said. "Or one of those grabber things that you use to pick of screws when you drop them inside an engine in a car."

Dr. Russel slowly pulled the scope back out. Bob sneezed a few times, and I felt his pain. That had to be an annoying sensation. Just thinking about it made the inside of my forehead itch.

"Coke!" Dr. Russel said suddenly. Everyone looked at her. "I saw someone use Coca-Cola on a choke in my internship, and it dissolved it. We need a bottle of Coke."

"There's a two-liter in my car," Stacey said. "I can run out and grab that."

I took the lead rope from her and she hurried out to her car. While we waited, Dr. Russel and Jessica cleaned the scope and put it back in the case. Stacey returned with the Coke, and everyone gathered back at the horse.

"How do you want to do this?" Stacey asked.

Dr. Russel pointed at the bucket. "Grab another clean bucket. We'll pour the Coke in there and add a bit of water to it. You pump it in just like water. Bring that one too, though. Once we clear it, we'll flush him out with water."

She grabbed the NG tube and set about putting it back in place. Bob shook his head and snorted, and my heart went out to him. This had to be getting old for him. When the tube hit the blockage, Jessica started pumping the Coke in.

"Hold up," Dr. Russel said. "We'll start there and let it sit for a minute."

I was doubtful that it would eat through the mass of shavings. Coke will do some amazing things, especially when it comes to cleaning and degreasing, but breaking down a mass of bedding, and whatever else was in his throat, seemed like a stretch. Water and Coke dribbled out of Bob's other nostril and pooled on the floor.

Dr. Russel probed the blockage with the tube, gently pushing against it. "Okay, give me a few more pumps."

Jessica worked the pump handle again, and the level of Coke in the bucket dropped another inch. We waited.

"Even if this doesn't work, the pump will be all cleaned up on the inside," I said. "We've got that going for us."

Dr. Russel probed the mass again, and suddenly the tube slid deeper into Bob's nose. "Yes!" Dr. Russel said with a grin. "Coke to the rescue!"

I stepped back out of the stall, knowing what was about to happen. With the blockage coming apart, Coke, water, bedding and food began pouring out of both nostrils. Bob shook his head and sneezed a few times, spraying everyone inside the stall with a mist of goo.

"Switch to straight water," Dr. Russel said. "Pump it slow and steady."

Jessica pulled the pump out of the Coke and stuck it in the water. I watched the water as it pushed the Coke through the clear tube and disappeared inside Bob's nose. The mess coming out of there gradually turned clear, with less and less solid material in it. Dr. Russel slowly fed the tube all the way down to his stomach. Bob was likely a bit dehydrated by this time, so they gave him the remaining water in the bucket.

"That was pretty slick," I said from the stall door as Dr. Russel removed the tube. "I really didn't think it would work."

Dr. Russel laughed. "I didn't know if it would or not, but it was worth a shot. Nothing else was working."

I could never be a doctor. My risk tolerance is so low that I couldn't experiment with something like that without knowing that it was very likely to succeed. Dr. Russel's confidence and experience gave her the ability to do what needed to be done for Bob, and it was humbling to consider that Bob would still be choking if it had been up to me to fix him. I'm just not wired for it. Fortunately for the horses, they're surrounded by amazing women who can get the job done. I'll stick to the bookkeeping, where the numbers always work out in the end.

Chapter 16

The Recipe for Disaster

I woke up from a ridiculous dream and rolled over, squinting to make out the time on the alarm clock: 2:33 am. I lay back with a sigh. After a dream like that, I'd really been hoping it was after 4:00 am, so I could just get up for the day. Since it was too early for that, I settled for a quick trip to the bathroom and a glass of water. That's usually enough to clear my dreams away so I can get back to sleep.

Erica shifted slightly as I slid back into bed. She's such a light sleeper that it's almost impossible to avoid waking her up, and I always feel guilty about it. I needn't have bothered being quiet, as it turned out. As soon as I got settled, her phone rang.

"Who in the world is up looking at their horses at this time of day?" I asked.

She grabbed her phone. "Hello?" I could tell she was groggy, as she didn't even give her name as she normally does.

The man's voice coming from her phone was clearly audible in the silence of the bedroom. He was exceptionally professional, and I knew in an instant that we were going to work.

"Is this Dr. Erica Lacher with Springhill Equine Veterinary Clinic?"

She sat up and swung her feet to the floor. "Yes, that's me."

"This is Sergeant John Hayes at the Florida State Police barracks in Jacksonville. We have a vehicle accident involving a horse trailer with two horses. The trailer is on its side in a ditch in East Palatka, and the horses are trapped inside. Can you respond to this?"

"Yes, of course."

I was already out of bed, pulling on clothes as fast as I could, as Erica wrote down the details. East Palatka was an hour and a half away, and if there were horses lying injured in a trailer waiting for us, every minute counted. By 2:39 am, we were in the vet truck, flying down the driveway.

As I have mentioned before, driving at night is always scary, as there are loads of animals out and about. I normally drive slower at night so that I can negotiate the hazards safely, as we all know that the safest place for an animal to be is on the opposite side of the road from wherever it is now. This truism covers the entire animal kingdom with the exception of squirrels, which are never sure which side is really safer. This was a special occasion, so I sent a silent plea out to the universe to keep the critters off the roads and put the gas pedal on the floor.

There's no good way to get to the east side of Gainesville from Newberry without going through town, with its endless string of traffic lights. We decided 39th Avenue was our best bet. At this hour, traffic was almost nonexistent, and nearly all the lights stayed green in our favor. The speed limit was 45mph, so I tried to keep it under 65mph going through town. I had my speech ready in case we got pulled over, but we didn't see any police. That was good. I'm not actually sure if an invitation from the state troopers was a license to speed or not, and I really didn't think it would keep us out of jail if I was super-speeding. It's a tough position to be in. I ran the two red lights we encountered, after making sure the intersections were clear.

The road between Gainesville and Palatka has a few tiny towns along the way, all the kind you would miss if you blinked. It's lined with forests and swamps, and is essentially a wild place. I stopped counting deer when I got to twenty, as it was unnerving. The speedometer hovered around 85, which is about as fast as the Pilot can safely go with all the vet gear in the back end. My heart rate hovered around 150, which was also probably as high as it could safely maintain. I rationalized the situation by telling myself that the faster we go, the less time the deer have to register our approach and cross the road, thus reducing our risk of hitting one. It made sense in my head at the time.

We passed a surprising number of cars headed into Gainesville. It was after 3:00 am by this time, so I guessed that it was approaching shift change time at one of the hospitals or something. I didn't spend much time thinking about it until one of them flipped on the strobe lights. It was a cop.

"Shit!" I said, hitting the brakes. I was doing 88 in a 55. "We don't have time for this." Maybe he heard me, or maybe he just didn't want to go through the hassle of pulling me over, but he shut the lights off and kept going towards Gainesville. I sent a silent *thank you* his direction and sped back up, hoping we wouldn't pass another one. Between the deer and the police, it felt like the deck was stacked against us.

Either the Universe provided, or my physics concept proved accurate. Either way, we made it to Palatka without hitting anything, or getting pulled over. I was much more cautious driving through Palatka, as it was 4:00 am by then, and there was a lot more traffic. We crossed the St. John's River and entered East Palatka.

"Okay, get ready to turn left on 207," Erica said. "It should be a big intersection."

"Got it." As we rounded a curve, the signs came into view. I put my signal on and eased into the turn lane. "How far out are we?"

"It's hard to say," Erica said. "The GPS doesn't recognize the address they gave us. The road is only a mile away, though."

I made the left turn. After a few blocks, town abruptly ended. We passed a patch of trees, and when they opened up into the flat fields of farmland, there was no question about where we were going. At least fifteen police cars, fire trucks, special emergency response vehicles, technical rescue trucks and trailers, and wreckers were lined up, and the collection of strobe lights lit up the sky and surrounding countryside like Christmas. Perhaps that's a bad analogy, as it was only two days after Christmas. It was impossible to miss.

I turned left onto the road, and immediately understood how the accident could happen. The road ran between two fields and was flanked by irrigation ditches on both sides. It was extremely narrow, and had undoubtedly been a private farm road when it was built. At some point it got paved and became a county road, but there was no shoulder at all. The asphalt dropped straight off into the irrigation ditches. If your trailer tire even flirted with the idea of going off the edge, such as it might if you were passing someone coming the other way, it could suck you right over the edge. It was a terrible road design.

I parked behind a fire truck and we jumped out. Erica opened the liftgate and I held the tray as she tossed in handfuls of needles and vials of drugs. We took off running a second later. It was about two hundred yards to the front of the line of emergency vehicles, and I had a hard time seeing where I was going with all the flashing lights. Driving past them at night is bad enough, but I was getting dizzy trying to run beside them. I kept my eyes on the white line at the edge of the pavement and followed Erica.

We passed the last fire truck and arrived at the scene of the accident. It was hard to make sense of what we were looking at. An old Ford pickup with a camper shell lay on its side in the ditch on the right side of the road, the driver's side tires just touching the asphalt. A bumper-pull two-horse trailer was behind it, also sideways. A group of people were in the ditch, which ran thigh-deep in water. Most of them were cutting the trailer apart, handing chunks of metal up to people in the field a piece at a time. There was a gray horse laying in the ditch behind the trailer, half-submerged in the water. There was a dog leash around his neck, and a deputy stood on the edge of the ditch above him, trying to hold his nose up out of the water. A knot of people stood in the road, waiting to assist in whatever way they could. Most of them held flashlights, pointing them at the trailer so the crew down there could see.

"Holy shit," I muttered. There was a whinny and the

sounds of hoofs scrabbling against metal from inside the trailer. No one paid much attention to us, so I called out loudly. "Veterinarian on scene. Who's in charge?"

One of the guys in the ditch looked up at me. "Hey, doc. The other vet just gave this one a shot. He's up front trying to get a look at the one inside. There's a ladder in front of the truck to get across the ditch."

I was surprised to hear that another veterinarian was there. From the looks of things, we were going to need a team of vets to manage this, so I was glad that we weren't going to be handling things alone. I couldn't tell what condition the horses were in, of course, but from the looks of the trailer, there were bound to be challenges getting them out of the trailer and out of the ditch. The fact that the gray horse was lying in the ditch, rather than standing, was telling.

A firefighter in full coat and helmet stepped up and guided us around the front of the truck. A narrow ladder had been placed across the ditch as a makeshift bridge.

"Hands and knees is the best way to cross," he said. "We're working on something better."

"We'll be okay," I said. Erica was already scooting across the ladder. I followed right behind her, awkwardly scrambling with one hand, as I had the tray in the other. The ladder sagged a bit under my weight, but I made it safely across and hurried to catch up with Erica.

There was a large piece of the trailer roof and side cut away on the front end, and a man squatted there, shining a flashlight inside. We stopped behind him and peered in over his shoulder. A big bay draft horse lay in the nose of the trailer, her head propped up against the floor behind her. The center divider covered her rump, and a big piece of grating lay on top of that. My best guess was that it used to go across the front of the stalls.

"Looks like we've got a mess here," Erica said. The man glanced up at her, and she introduced us. "I'm Dr. Lacher, from Springhill Equine Veterinary Clinic. This is my husband, Justin. Are you the other vet?"

He stood up and extended his hand. He was tall and slender, with dark hair that was graying at the temples. "Yeah, hello. I'm Bert Grayson, their primary veterinarian."

"Have you been able to do anything yet?" Erica asked, quickly shaking his hand.

"I just got some Banamine into Chief," he said, gesturing at the back of the trailer. "I've only been here a few minutes, myself. Chief can't stand up, so I didn't push him on that. Babe, here, doesn't have any obvious things going on, but she's fighting pretty hard. I was just trying to figure out how to get some sedation in her."

As if on cue, Babe lunged at the opening cut into the roof, but her hooves just slid on the front wall of the trailer, unable to gain any traction. The metal panels covering her lower half would prevent her from making any progress anyway, even if she could fit out the hole.

"I've got drugs right here," Erica said. "I don't know how we're going to get a vein on her, though, the way she's moving around."

"I'll hold you up by the belt," I said. "I think you can get a foot on that divider and lean down to her, and I'll hold you up from here."

She switched on her headlamp and grabbed a needle out of the tray. "It's the best we've got. If I have to, I can give it to her in the muscle. It'll take longer, but it's better than nothing.

Are you good with that?"

Dr. Grayson nodded. "Do it."

I stepped to the back of the trailer to talk to the guy in charge. They were doing a battery change on what I assumed were the Jaws of Life, so it was relatively quiet for a moment.

"Hey guys, we're going to put a vet in the trailer and try to sedate the horse in there. Can you give us a minute?"

"Yeah, go for it. St. John's County just got here, and they've got all the right tools for this stuff. We'll talk this out once you get the horse drugged and make a new plan." He made his way to the edge of the ditch, and I went back to the front of the trailer. Erica had the drugs pulled up and was waiting with Dr. Grayson.

"Ready?"

She nodded, and stuck the syringe between her teeth, grabbing the sides of the trailer. I grabbed the back of her pants, clenching my fist around her belt.

"Be careful of the sharp edges," I said. The sheet metal was sheared off in multiple pieces, leaving a multitude of razor-sharp points around the edge of the hole. I wished for a pair of gloves as I braced myself and lowered her inside. I could see pretty well once she was in, as the guys at the back of the trailer shined their lights inside for her. Someone came up beside me and shined a light in from the front.

Erica got one foot on the center divider and tested the surface. It was slanted down and away from us and wasn't connected to the floor on the front end. The rescue guys had already attached a cable to it when they cut the front of the trailer out, and the cable was holding it up, so the weight wasn't on the horse. It was twisted on the back end, and that was what they were working on when we got there.

"Is this cable attached to something sturdy?" Erica shouted.

"Yeah, you're good," someone at the back called out. "It's the winch cable on the truck. It'll hold."

I could tell she was nervous, and I tried not to think about how dangerous this was. There was no way to give the horse a shot to relax her without being in striking range of the head and the front feet. I wasn't strong enough to just yank her out with one arm if the horse panicked. I could help, but it would be up to Erica to jump back.

With one foot firmly on the panel and braced against the cable, she leaned forward. I held more and more of her weight as she reached across the space to brace herself on the floorboards across from us, which were now the side instead of the floor. Babe lifted her head up, and Erica put her other hand on Babe's nose, shushing her.

"It's okay, mama. I'm here to help you out. Just be calm, let me get this shot into you." The words were hard to make out around the needle in her mouth, but her tone was soothing and calm. She grabbed the needle, pulling the cap off with her teeth. Reaching down, she ran her thumb along Babe's neck, trying to locate the vein. With Babe's head being turned up like it was, the vein wasn't as easy to see as it normally would be. She stuck the needle in, pulling the plunger back with her thumb to see if she was in the vein. No luck. She repositioned, and Babe jerked her head, forcing Erica to pull the needle out as I yanked her back.

"Easy, Babe," Erica said. "Easy, big girl. Lower me back down."

I eased her down again. Babe lay back, blowing air out her nose in great gusts. It's hard for horses to breathe when they're laying down, as their guts put a lot of pressure on their lungs.

All her struggling was using up oxygen, making it worse. It was imperative that Erica get the drugs into her to calm her down.

Babe was still until the needle went in again, then she lunged up. I hauled Erica back, straining to keep her ahead of Babe.

"Okay, one more time," Erica said. "I'm just going to give it in the muscle, unless you want to try." She glanced at Dr. Grayson.

"No, it's not going to happen," he said. "She's too stressed out."

I lowered Erica in again. She stuck the needle in Babe's shoulder, quickly pushing the plunger down. Babe lay still, and I pulled Erica back out of the trailer, covering her head with my hand to keep her from scalping herself. She handed me the needle, and we walked to the back of the trailer.

"It's going to take a few minutes for the drugs to kick in," she said. "Do you guys have a plan?"

"We're about to make one. Hang tight."

Several firefighters were placing another ladder across the ditch behind the trailer, just beyond Chief. They laid a 2 x 6 board on top of the ladder, and as soon as it was in place, several men crossed it as the man in the ditch climbed up the steep embankment to join us. Introductions were brief.

"Bob Millhouse, Putnam County Fire Rescue."

"Jim Lambert, St. John's County Technical Rescue. What's the situation?"

"We've got the trailer doors cut away. This horse here was on top, and he got himself out of the trailer, but he can't get up. There's another horse inside, trapped under the divider. We're trying to figure out how to cut it out of there without dropping it on her, and without leaving metal behind that could slice her up when we pull her out. These are the veterinarians, and they just got sedatives into the horse in the trailer."

"Okay, how do you want to do this? We've got the trailer here with all the gear, and three trucks."

"You guys have all the tools and the training," Bob said. "If you want to take point, we'll provide support and manpower. We need light, and we need a way to get this horse out of the ditch."

Jim turned to the road and shouted at someone standing there. "Wilson, get these vehicles moved. Get the light tower up front so we can see, and put the trailer right behind it. We're going to need the ropes and straps."

I crossed the ladder bridge, which was much easier with the board on it, and jogged back down to the vet truck. There was a state trooper car right behind me, so I couldn't back up. I waited to see what everyone else was doing. This was a task that would have taken thirty minutes in other places that I've worked, like the Army, but within two minutes, all the vehicles were over in the left lane. Two of the fire trucks up front backed down the right lane, which was an incredibly tight squeeze, and in the dark, no less. I stood behind the vet truck, cringing as they went by, but they made it safely to the back. A moment later, a different fire truck came by, headed for the front. It was followed by another truck with a big trailer. I followed them to the front.

Firefighters swarmed the trailer, gathering tools and supplies, so I waited behind them, out of the way. I could see Erica across the way. She and Dr. Grayson were squatting above Chief, trying to examine him. The sound of hydraulics caught my attention, and I looked around for the source of it. The fire truck in front was the source, at least according to my ears, but I couldn't tell what was happening. A small red light appeared above the truck, and I squinted to make it out. It looked like a mast was raising from the fire truck, but that didn't make sense.

A moment later, the bank of intensely bright floodlights at the top of it came to life, and I understood. A cheer went up from the workers in the ditch, as it was suddenly daylight.

I crossed the bridge and went over to Erica. She turned as I approached, and stood up, stretching her back.

"I need the rope halter out of the truck. It should be on the left side of the box. We've got a lead rope here, but the halter's broken."

"Got it." I turned and re-crossed the bridge and ran back to the truck. This was my second trip back already, and I had a feeling that I was going to be a master of the 200-yard dash before the night was over. The halter was right where it was supposed to be, and I hurried back up front, reminding myself to thank our techs for keeping the trucks organized.

Dr. Grayson was standing in the water when I got back, holding Chief's head up. I handed the halter to Erica, and she passed it down to him. Together, they lifted Chief's massive draft head and worked the halter in place. They were very careful passing it over his right eye, which was swollen to the size of a plum. I wasn't sure it would fit him, but it did. Fortunately, he was on the small end of the draft horse spectrum. He was big, but he wasn't Clydesdale big. Erica handed me the lead rope.

"Keep his nose out of the water so he doesn't drown."

I nodded. Beside me, a pickup was driving across the muddy field. Having witnessed a technical horse rescue once before, I guessed that this would be the anchor vehicle for the block and tackle system they would use to pull the horses out of the ditch. Firefighters began pouring across the bridge carrying equipment over to the truck.

While the complicated rope and pulley system was being set up, the other team was back in the ditch, cutting the trailer apart with the Hurst hydraulic cutting tool. Back when I was a kid, they called this the Jaws of Life, but it's evolved quite a bit since those days. They stopped several times to discuss the structural integrity of the shell, and what would happen if this cross brace was removed, or that axle. It was impressive to see the Hurst tool itself in action. It's essentially a pair of scissors with stubby blades and a battery-powered hydraulic system to open and close it. It will cut through nearly anything, and these guys were putting it to the test.

Erica tapped me on the leg, and I realized she'd said my name several times. The noise level was tremendous with all the diesel engines running on the fire trucks, the radios crackling, and the guys cutting the trailer apart. I glanced down, and she waved me out of the way so she could stand up. Jim was back with two other guys.

"Okay," Jim said. "We need to get some straps around this guy. We usually put one right behind the front legs and one in front of the back legs. Does that sound good? No injuries in those areas we need to avoid?"

"Not that we can tell," Erica said. "It's going to be tough to get the straps under him, though. Do you have a flat bar?"

"Yeah, we've got all that stuff."

"Okay, tell me when you're ready, and we'll sedate him."

"We're five minutes out," Jim said.

Erica nodded. "Justin, grab the tray. I'll hold his head."

I handed her the lead rope and ran back to the front of the trailer. The tray was sitting by a pile of shovels and scrap metal that used to be the roof. I was back in a few seconds, and Erica grabbed a syringe and began drawing up drugs as soon as I took the rope from her.

Bob stepped over from the ditch where he was guiding

the dismantling of the trailer. "How long until we get this horse moved?"

"They're four minutes out," Erica said. "We're about to sedate him."

"Okay," Bob said. "We can't do much more until he's out of the way. We need this space."

Erica gave him the thumbs up, and he went back to his crew. "Okay, listen up," he shouted. "They're about ready to haul that horse out of the ditch. Let's get everyone up there to lend a hand on the ropes. Everybody, let's go."

They scrambled up the bank of the ditch, one at a time. The first one up turned to extend a hand to the others, pulling them up. It must have been tough wearing the heavy firefighter pants and coat, and the huge rubber boots. The ditch was about five feet deep, and the walls were steep and muddy. I was impressed with the physicality of the firefighters, as well as the positive attitude they displayed about everything.

Erica handed the syringe to Dr. Grayson, and he quickly administered the shot. Chief rolled his eye up to watch them, but he made no attempt to move. I felt like that wasn't good, even though it made life much easier on everyone. Babe's struggling against the shot made things difficult, but at least we knew she was an active participant in what was going on. They had both been lying in place for nearly three hours at this point, and that's bad for a horse.

Jim came back with another guy, and they scrambled down the wall to Chief. Jim was carrying what had to be the flat bar Erica had asked about. It looked like a leaf spring from a car, a long flat piece of spring steel with a T handle on one end. He slid the end behind Chief's shoulder and shoved it down. The other man got down in the water and walked up to Chief's belly.

"Oh, that's a really dangerous place to be," Dr. Grayson said. He was back in the water too, holding Chief's head up to keep him still. "If he kicks, he could break your leg."

"We've got to get a strap under him," the man said. "We'll just hope those drugs do the trick. Let's go."

Jim pushed down on the handle again, driving it further beneath Chief. The fireman in the water stuck his arm under Chief's submerged belly, feeling for the bar.

"I got nothing, boss."

"We're probably in the mud," Jim said. "Let me reset." He yanked on the handle until the bar came free and tried again a few inches away. The bar slid smoothly beneath the horse for about a foot before Jim had to start wiggling it between thrusts.

The guy in the ditch had his coat off and was up to his shoulder in the water as he felt for the other end of the bar. "Still nothing."

"I can't get it any further down," Jim grunted. "Let's use the hose." He pulled the bar back out and shouted to someone up on the road. "Hose pipe! We gotta blast a path. Let's go!"

People sprang into action, and a few seconds later a water hose came down the embankment. On the end, a stiff but flexible tube was attached. Jim grabbed it and stuck it in the hole he'd created with the bar.

"Water on!" he shouted.

"Water on," came the return cry. The other end of the hose was attached to an outlet on the bumper of the big fire truck with the light tower. The fireman there turned on the faucet, and the hose jumped under the pressure.

I've seen this technique used with water wells, but it never would have occurred to me to use it to bore a tunnel under a horse. Jim bent the tube slightly as he fed it under Chief an inch at a time. After a minute, he pulled it back out. "Water off!"

"Water off," came the return cry.

He grabbed the bar again and shoved it down in the hole. It went most of the way to the handle before it met serious resistance this time. He shoved, and the guy in the water felt around, pulling handfuls of mud away as he searched for it. Finally, he shouted in triumph. "Got it! Keep going."

Jim leaned on the handle, forcing the bar down with all his might. The handle was almost down to Chief's back. "That's about all we got."

"Okay, throw me a one-inch strap. We'll have to pull that through, and then use it to pull the big strap back under him."

Jim tossed an orange nylon strap down to him. The strap disappeared under the water as he fed it through the slot in the end of the bar. His fingers had to be wrinkled and prune-like by this time, and I couldn't imagine how Chief felt. He'd been in the water for hours. The guy in the water stood up, holding both ends of the strap.

"Okay, pull it through."

Jim pulled the bar back out, and the orange strap went with it. When it was clear on the other side, he tossed the bar out of the way and grabbed the end of the six-inch wide strap that another fireman stood by holding. He tied the two straps together.

While Jim did that, the guy in the water was working with the people up on the road. They fed a winch cable down from the front of the fire truck and hooked it to the orange strap. When everyone was ready, they began winching the strap through the hole under Chief. It went smooth, and a moment later, the front strap was in position.

The second strap went much easier. Jim started with the hose and blasted a path under Chief's flanks. It took another five minutes to get the straps in place and connected to the block and tackle, but at last, it was time to get Chief out of the ditch. I got back out of the way, and Erica moved to the side to help Dr. Grayson manage Chief's head.

"Let's get the sled in here," Jim shouted. Two guys appeared with a big piece of stiff plastic, about the size of a sheet of plywood. They slid it under the straps and wedged it under Chief's back.

"Shovels," one of them shouted. "Let's cut the top of this bank back so it's not so steep."

I thought it would take forever, but the four guys and one woman that jumped into action with shovels had the top of the ditch cut away in seconds. I decided that they must spend a lot of time in the gym. Five seconds of shoveling that fast with all that gear on would have killed me. Did I mention that it was hot and humid? It might have been late December, but it was t-shirt weather. This is Florida.

They set the shovels aside and ran back to the ropes. It was a complicated array of ropes and pulleys that stretched back and forth between the truck in the field and the horse. There was a line of about ten people on each side holding the ends of the rope. It looked like a game of adult tug of war was about to take place, except that everyone was pulling the same direction. One man stood in front to call out commands to the pulling team.

"Ready!" he shouted.

Jim stood beside the horse and shouted back after double-checking everything. "Ready!"

"Pull rope!"

Everyone heaved on the ropes, and Chief began inching up the wall onto the piece of plastic. It began moving with him, and I jumped over to brace it. Jim held the other side. Erica and Dr. Grayson struggled to keep his head help up until it was on the plastic, so he didn't end up with an eye ulcer on top of everything else.

As Chief's lower body and legs came out of the water, I saw why he hadn't tried to stand up. His right hind leg was flopping loosely at the fetlock joint. There were several lacerations visible in the harsh white light, and I cringed, thinking about the infection risk of having been submerged in an irrigation ditch.

Once the horse was over the top of the ditch, everything went much easier. The plastic sled had straps tied through the hand holes, and I grabbed one to help keep it underneath him, following Jim's lead.

"Keep going," Jim shouted. "As far as you can go."

A few seconds later, it was over. They unhooked the ropes and pulled the straps back out, and the demolition crew went back to the trailer to start the next phase.

"We need to get him off the sled," Erica said. "He won't be able to stand up on it, and once he wakes up, we've got to get him on his feet."

I pointed to his fetlock. "Do you think he'll be able to stand with that?"

Erica shrugged. "Maybe. Probably. It might just be a severed tendon, which isn't that serious."

It looked serious to me, but I'm not the doctor. Everyone grabbed a handle or a strap and pulled on the sled. Erica held his head while Dr. Grayson held his tail, and the sled slid neatly out from under him.

A whinny and the crashing of hooves on metal drew my attention back to the trailer, and I ran over to the hole in the front. Babe was coming out of the sedation, and she was desperate to move. My heart went out to her, and I knew she had to be numb from lying there on the same side for so long. I stuck my hand out and spoke softly to her while Erica drew up another shot.

"Easy, Babe. Easy, girl. We're working hard to get you out of there, I promise. I know it hurts. Just hang in there."

Babe looked at me, then looked over her shoulder at the back of the trailer, as if to tell me that she needed to get out. The communication barrier wasn't keeping us from understanding one another in terms of needs, but I had no way to explain to her how hard it was to get her out of there. The technical rescue teams train for this kind of thing, and even they were struggling to get the mission accomplished quickly.

Erica tapped me on the shoulder. "Let me in."

I moved to the side and grabbed her by the belt as she stepped into the hole. "Hopefully she'll let you get a vein this time."

"I doubt it. She's hurting too bad." She stuck the syringe between her teeth and grabbed the top of the opening. "Okay, let's go. Slow." I could hardly understand the words, but I knew what she meant.

Babe lunged again and again as Erica got her foot into position on the divider. The effort was moving her even further into the nose of the trailer. Her head and neck were almost vertical against the front wall. She flexed her lower front leg, bending it as far as she could. I knew how she felt. If I sit in one position too long and I can't move, such as on a long bus ride with my luggage on my lap, my legs go crazy. She had that times a thousand because of the immense amount of weight she carried, on top of the bruises and injuries she'd sustained from the crash itself. I wanted so bad to snap my fingers and teleport her out of there, and my helplessness was infuriating. That's not something I'm good at. I like to solve problems, but all I could do was try to help the professionals and soothe the horse as much as I could.

Erica didn't even try for a vein this time. Babe was too distraught to stay still for it, and the further she moved from the center divider, the harder it was for Erica to reach her. At this point, the only way to get to her neck would be to sit on her shoulder, and that was out of the question. Erica gave her the shot quickly, then sat for a moment and stroked her withers, trying to comfort her.

"You about done in there, doc?" a voice came in from the back.

"Yep, I'm coming out." I lifted her by the belt and guided her hand to a safe place on the edge of the hole, and she climbed out.

"Let's get this roof cut away," Bob shouted. "I need everybody holding on to something. We can't let this fall into the trailer."

Erica and I scrambled back out of the way as the guys jumped into position. There was a guy on each end of the trailer with a Hurst cutting tool, and they began working their way towards the center, cutting big chunks of the roof away. Next, they went to the other side and cut through the floorboard in the center, severing the mounts for the center divider. With the roof out of the way, they were able to use straps and the winch cable to keep the divider from falling on Babe, and they quickly maneuvered it out the back of the trailer.

Bob and Jim came over to talk to Erica and Dr. Grayson. They were both covered in mud, and sweat ran down their faces, leaving streaks in the grime.

"Okay, Doc. What are you thinking?"

Erica looked at Dr. Grayson, then down at Babe. "We've

got to knock her out in order to get a strap around her, and I have to get in the vein to do that. Can you cut me a hole behind her head somehow, so I can get to her from the other side?"

Jim studied the scene for a moment. "Even with her being out cold, we won't be able to get a strap around her the way she's up against the side like that."

Bob nodded. "What do you think about cutting the trailer in half down the other side? We can put the winches on it and pull it back as we go. Then we'll have better access to her."

Jim clapped his hands once. "That's a plan. Let's do it. Doc, how's she doing on sedation? Do you need to hit her again before we do this?"

Erica shook her head. "Not yet. I'll let you know if that changes."

Bob and Jim began giving orders and getting their teams into position for the next phase of the rescue. I realized with a start that the sun was coming up. Babe had been in the same spot for over five hours, now. The end was in sight, but that's way too long. If I hadn't been there to witness the incredible difficulty of the task, I might have been critical of how long it took to extract them, but there were few places that more than a minute or two could have been saved. It was just a monumental task.

I made my way across the ladder to see how they were going to do this. I had to stay back, as they had a winch cable from each of the closest fire trucks hooked onto the top of the trailer. I was imagining they would need a cutting torch or something to get through the axles, but much to my surprise, the Hurst sliced right through them. I made a mental note to leave an Amazon review for Hurst.

With the axles cut in half, the winch cables were tightened.

The driver's side wall, which was currently the roof, began to fold back.

"Easy, easy," Jim shouted. "Let off a bit. Let's get some straps on this thing before you start cutting."

Nylon straps were quickly secured to the ends of the wall, and the cutting team got into position. They started at the center, cutting the support beams that ran across the floor of the trailer, and worked their way out. As they started cutting the outside beams, the whole side of the trailer wall and floor began to slowly fold back down to the road.

"Winch in," Jim shouted. "Keep the tension on it. Tight on those straps. Guide it down, boys, and watch the cutters."

The trailer tires, which had been overhead, slowly drifted down to the asphalt, pulling the side wall with them. I ran back across the ladder bridge to grab the tray and help Erica, but she and Dr. Grayson were already crossing the other bridge in front of the truck when I got there. I instantly felt guilty for gawking instead of working, but it was too late, now. I glanced over at Chief to see if I could do anything there, but he was still asleep. His owner stood beside him, watching. I turned back to the trailer.

Erica was talking to one of the firefighters. I couldn't hear her, but she was making hand gestures, explaining something. A moment later, he made another cut on the front of the trailer and pulled the sheet metal back. Erica stepped into the gap, just behind Babe's head. Dr. Grayson stood right behind her, ready.

The firefighter at the front waved his arms and shouted to the crew in the back. "Are we ready to sedate?"

Bob and Jim were both in the ditch, up to their thighs in the water. Behind them, the rest of the rescue crew was lined up. Some held straps, some held big body boards, and some were shoveling more of the embankment away to create a better angle to slide Babe up the wall. After a quick check, Jim gave them a thumbs up. "Go for sedation!"

Erica was patting Babe on the neck, trying to keep her calm. She slowly leaned in, and I stopped breathing. She was surrounded by sheet metal with jagged edges, and if she jerked back to avoid Babe, she could be seriously hurt. Babe didn't move, and Erica slowly worked her hand around the big vein in the neck, clamping a thumb across it. A moment later she had the needle in the vein and delivered the all-important drugs. I let out a sigh as Erica stood back.

"Two minutes," she shouted to Jim, holding up two fingers. "Give it two minutes."

I moved down the ditch so I could hear the discussion between Jim and Bob. They had much better access to Babe now, but I still didn't know exactly how this was going to work.

"The strap's got to go over her back, and come around between her back legs," Jim was saying. "Once she's knocked out, I think we can rock her hips enough to get the strap under her without using the flat bar. It'll go a lot faster that way."

"Sounds good to me," Bob said. "Maybe we can work a sled under her at the same time."

Jim nodded. "Get a sled up here," he shouted.

One of the guys on the ropes team came over to stand beside me. "I don't see why the horse can't just stand up and walk out."

"She can't stand up," I said. "She's been lying on her side for five hours. Because they're so heavy, all the blood gets squeezed out of their muscles when they're lying like this. She's totally numb on the left side of her body."

His eyes widened in surprise. "Damn. That's probably not good."

"It's not good at all," I said. "Tissue can only go so long without oxygen before it starts dying."

I could see the realization crossing his face. "So even if she wasn't hurt too bad in the crash, just lying there could kill her?"

"Yeah, if she's there too long. Horses weren't meant to lay down for more than an hour. Their bodies just can't handle it."

He fell silent. We watched as Erica checked Babe for responsiveness and gave Jim the all clear. Jim hoisted himself onto the remains of the trailer, pausing as it shifted slightly under his weight. When it stopped, he cautiously climbed to his feet, searching for traction on the sloping trailer wall.

"Palmer, get me a handful of extraction blankets," he called out. "We need to cover all these sharp edges before we start moving her around."

Bob tossed a six-inch strap inside and hauled himself up beside Jim, holding on to him as he got to his feet. "Woo, boy, this is going to be fun." He worked his way around Babe's hindquarters until he was opposite Jim. They unrolled the strap and stretched it out.

Suddenly, Chief let out a long whinny. I glanced over to see him sitting up.

"He's waking up," Dr. Grayson said. "I'll go manage Chief, if you've got this. I want to keep him down as long as I can." Erica agreed, and he ran to the ladder bridge and hurried across. Chief dropped his head back to the ground, and Dr. Grayson knelt by his neck, holding his head down. Chief needed time for the drugs to wear off before he stood up, especially with his fetlock hanging. It was important for him to stand up, but not too soon.

"Give me two more people in here," Bob said. I spun back around, making eye contact with Erica to see if she needed me to do anything. She mimed looking at her watch and shook her head. We both knew it was taking too long, despite the heroic efforts of everyone on the scene.

With four sets of hands, it only took a minute to get the strap under Babe's hindquarters. The blankets were in place on the jagged edges, and they jammed the big sheet of plastic under her flanks.

"Hook up the strap, and let's get on the ropes," Bob shouted. "One minute to pull!"

Things were happening fast. I felt like a dolt just standing there watching, but there was no place for me to pitch in. I reminded myself again that I was there to help Erica, and that made me feel a little better, but I'm not very good at standing around.

"Ready?" Jim stood inside the trailer, holding one of the straps on the sled to keep it still. Another strap lay on the floor, but I couldn't reach it from the outside.

"Jim," I shouted, pointing at the strap. "Toss me that strap."

He grabbed the end of the strap and threw it across to me, then positioned himself so he wouldn't get caught in Babe's legs. "Pull rope!"

"Pull rope," the call echoed out.

Babe began to creep backwards onto the sled. At the end of the trailer, a crew held sheets of plywood, braced with 2 x 8 lumber, as a makeshift bridge between the trailer and the bank. It was jammed into the mud wall on one side, but they would be holding her weight on the other side. I braced myself as the sled tried to pull the strap out of my hands.

Once Babe was on the sled, I ran to the back of the trailer to help keep it underneath her. She slid off the trailer and onto the makeshift bridge. I could see the men straining to hold the board up as she passed by, their jaws set in grim determination. Maybe there's something to that whole 'fire-fighters are heroes' thing. Those guys were impressive.

"Go, go, go!" Jim shouted. "Don't stop!"

The end of the sled reached the dirt and started up the slope. This put Babe on an angle, and I was afraid that her head and upper body might slide over into the water, but Jim's commands kept her moving right up the wall into the field. When we were about fifteen feet from the ditch, he called out to stop. I dropped the little strap I'd been holding and grabbed the big strap as soon as it was unhooked, pulling it through her leg and tossing it over her back.

"Good job, everybody." Jim and Bob shook hands. "That's one for the record books, there."

We pulled the sled out from under Babe and put a towel under her eyes, draping it across her face. Erica was on the other side of Babe, checking her over inch by inch for injuries. I stood by, ready to do whatever she needed. The Putnam County and St. John's County rescue teams began the long and arduous process of cleaning and stowing all their gear. Everything was covered in mud, but they had the advantage of high-pressure fire hoses to wash it all down, which made it easier.

I glanced over at Chief, who was off to our left. To my surprise, he was standing. Dr. Grayson held the lead rope in one hand, and was rubbing the muscles in Chief's legs where he'd been laying on them all night with the other. Chief was holding his injured foot up, but he was attempting to get the hoof in the right position, so he could lean on it.

"Look at that," I said to Erica. "He's trying to stand on it."

"Hopefully it's just a tendon," she said. "That's what it's looking like."

The owner of the horses had draped a blanket over Chief. It was off-white with red, green, yellow, and black stripes on it in a Native American design. It was fitting, as the owner was Native American, himself. Dr. Grayson took a few steps back, and to my surprise, Chief took a few steps forward. He was clumsy on his injured fetlock, but it only took him a moment to get the hang of swinging his leg forward and waiting a moment for his hoof to get into place before setting it down. They walked in a long, sweeping turn and came over near us.

"The county has a horse trailer down there," Dr. Grayson called, pointing to the other end of the field. "I'm going to see if I can get Chief out of here. Their farm is just down the road. Once I get him situated, I'll be back to help you out with her."

"Okay," Erica said. "We'll hold the fort down."

They slowly walked away, pausing to rest every twenty feet or so. Chief looked rough with his swollen eye and bum leg, but he soldiered down the field through the sunrise and disappeared behind the line of emergency vehicles. I hoped he would be able to get on the trailer, both from a physical and a psychological standpoint. After the night he's had, he had plenty of reasons to never get on another trailer. I could see a police car pull out onto the main road and stop traffic, and a moment later, a truck and horse trailer backed out into the intersection, and my questions were answered. Chief was done being here in the field, and was ready to go home, even if it meant another trailer ride.

It took another twenty minutes for Babe to begin stirring. Erica let her lay for a bit longer with her eyes covered. Their owner had brought a few buckets of water for Chief, and I helped him carry them over for Babe. Chief had finished half of the first bucket, but the other one was still full. When Babe was sternal, Erica pulled the towel off her eyes and we offered her the water.

Dr. Grayson returned about a half hour later. Babe was still down, despite Erica's best efforts to get her up. As he approached, Erica walked over to talk to him, out of earshot of the owner.

"It's not looking good," she said. "She's made some efforts to get up, but her left side just isn't functioning."

Dr. Grayson nodded, his face ashen. "She was down way too long. There's probably a lot of dead muscle in there."

"What do you want to do?" Erica asked.

"Let's try together, and see if we can stand her up," he said. "If we can help her up, she might have a chance. I can't throw in the towel without trying everything."

"I'm right there with you," Erica said. We turned back to Babe.

Dr. Grayson took her head, and Erica went to her tail. I positioned myself along her back side and began nudging her in the ribs with my knees. Erica pulled out her Leatherman and used the pliers to pinch Babe in her most sensitive area beneath her tail. I don't think there is any greater motivation to stand up than that, and I've seen Erica use it with great success on many horses who thought they couldn't stand up.

Babe lunged forward, her front end rising up briefly, but fell back. "Hold on," Dr. Grayson said. He grabbed her front feet, which were folded to one side, and pulled them out in front of her. Now there was one less thing she needed to do to stand up. "Okay, let's go again."

I banged my knees into her ribs and Erica pinched, smacking Babe's butt with her other hand.

"Come on, girl, up you go!" Dr. Grayson gave her plenty of slack in the lead rope, standing out in front of her so she had room to maneuver. Babe lunged forward again, blowing great gusts of air out her nostrils with the effort. She made it halfway up, her legs shaking violently with the effort. Erica rushed around to her other side, and together we pushed upwards on her hindquarters. Her legs straightened out, but the quivering continued. However, she was up, and that was huge progress.

"Good girl," Dr. Grayson said, patting her neck. He shared a glance with Erica. I could tell that it wasn't good from the look on their faces. Babe bent her knees, trying to lay back down, and he quickly stopped her. "No, no, no, you've got to stay up."

The owner stood nearby; his face drawn. I hadn't spent much time with him, or even thinking about what he must be going through. I didn't even know if he'd been the one driving the truck, or if it was the other guy there with him. Either way, his whole world was falling apart, and I felt guilty for not thinking about him sooner. He was older than me, somewhere in his fifties, a heavyset man with long black hair. His ballcap showed a military ribbon with the words, *Native Veteran* above it. He made eye contact with me for a moment, and I dropped my head. I had no idea what to say. He had to be exhausted, on top of everything else. I'd had five hours of sleep before we got here. He'd been in Jacksonville, driving a carriage all night.

A moment later, Babe went back down. Even lying flat out, her whole body shook violently. I didn't want to ask out loud, but it looked to me like she was having a seizure. Dr. Grayson waved the owner over, and we gathered in a circle beside Babe.

"I'm going to run her some IV fluids," Dr. Grayson said. "I don't think it's going to do much, but it's the only thing we have left."

"What's happening to her?" the owner asked.

"She's in shock," Dr. Grayson said. "She hasn't had any blood in the muscles on her left side in-" he checked his watch, "in about six hours. There's going to be a lot of dead tissue in there, releasing enzymes and toxins into her system. She's fighting that off while she's trying to repair the damage, and it's just too much. We're hoping that getting her up will get enough blood back into circulation to keep her alive. Running fluids will hydrate her a bit more, but it's a last-ditch effort."

"We have to try. She's given me everything. I owe it to her to give her everything."

Dr. Grayson turned to Erica. "There's not much else you can do here, if you need to go. I know you have a long drive home, and probably a full day of appointments waiting on you."

"Oh, the office is already shuffling the schedule around," Erica said. "But if you've got it under control, we'll go ahead and get rolling."

Dr. Grayson shook her hand. "Thank you so much for coming to help with this. If I ever have somebody on your side of the river in need of a vet, I'll point them to Springhill Equine."

Erica smiled. "Hey, this is what we do. You've got my number. Keep me posted on Babe and Chief."

We shook hands all around and gathered our stuff. The wrecker guys already had what was left of the trailer pulled out of the ditch, as well as the truck. They were loading the pieces of trailer that has been cut away onto a flatbed truck. Aside from the churned-up dirt, you'd never even know something happened here.

"The bridge is gone," Erica said.

I looked around. Sure enough, the rescue teams had

already pulled the ladders from the ditch, hosed them off, and put them away.

"We can walk down to the culvert," I said. "The vet truck is down there, anyway."

Back at the truck, we quickly sorted through the tray and the bucket. The used needles went in the sharps container, and most of the rest went in the trash. I looked at Erica. She was covered in mud, and the bags under her eyes told me she was exhausted. I probably didn't look much better.

"Let's go home, kid," I said. "We've got to get you a shower before you go to work." I thought about our morning routine, and it hit me like a hammer. "Oh shit, the horses! We need to call your mom and get her to bring them in and feed. I can't believe I forgot about that!"

I pulled my phone out of my pocket. I had a variety of missed messages and calls, several of them from Erica's mom.

Horses are in and fed. Are you coming back here at some point?

I let out a sigh of relief. It was after nine in the morning, and our critters are on a very consistent morning routine. They were probably on the verge of mutiny by the time they got breakfast.

"You mom was on it, today," I said. "She texted me at 8:30 that she fed. Hopefully they weren't too bad."

"That's a relief," Erica said. "We owe her for that one."

She slept most of the way home. I decided to stay closer to the speed limit, now that the crisis was over. With all the daytime traffic, I didn't have much choice anyway.

Later that afternoon, Erica sent me a text.

Dr. Grayson called. Babe didn't make it.

I let out a long breath. On some level, I felt like it was probably better that she didn't survive. The trauma to her muscles would have taken years to overcome, and her quality of life would not have been great during that process. Still, it was incredibly sad. Babe had put up a valiant fight. People from all over north central Florida had worked as hard as they could to save her. It was just a horrible situation.

I felt bad for Chief. He wasn't out of the woods yet, either, and he'd lost his work partner and friend. I knew that Dr. Grayson would do everything in his power to care for him, but you can't cure the sense of loss that Chief and his family were dealing with. The only thing for that is time.

I want to close this chapter by saying thanks to all the men and women in this world who have committed their lives to helping others in times of crisis. The amazing people from the Florida state police, the Putnam County deputies, and the Putnam County and St. John's County fire and rescue teams were incredible to witness in action. The long hours they spend training for things like this are generally thankless, and definitely grueling and difficult. They were presented with a situation that seemed hopeless to me, but they used their knowledge, experience, and resources to overcome the incredible difficulties, and extract the horses as safely and humanely as possible. Babe lost her life despite their best efforts, and sometimes it goes that way, but Chief lived because of their efforts, and he wouldn't have without them. These people are often invisible in society, but I would ask that the next time you see some police or firemen eating lunch somewhere, grab their waitress and pick up their tab. I promise you they've earned it.

Chapter 17

DOUBLE TROUBLE

ANOTHER SATURDAY MORNING, another colic. I know that horses have all kinds of injuries and illnesses, but sometimes it seems like all they ever do is colic. It's by far the most common emergency that we see. The other two that we get calls for a lot are abscesses and chokes, but we rarely have to see those. Erica is usually able to handle that kind of thing with a phone call.

This horse was one of our regular patients. I knew his owner, Carol, from our seminars, but I'd never been to their farm. That's usually a good thing, as it means they probably haven't had an emergency in a long time, or, at least, not when we were on call.

"Turn right on the next road," Erica said. "It's kind of hidden. Start slowing down."

I took my foot off the gas, trying to find a street sign in the trees up ahead. "I don't see it."

"Just keep slowing down."

Suddenly we were on top of the road, if you could call it that. Pine needles and leaves covered the faint tracks coming out of the trees, thoroughly disguising everything. I jammed on the brakes, but there was no way we were stopping in time. I stepped on the gas again.

"We'll have to find a place to turn around," I said. "Sorry about that."

"I told you to slow down," Erica said with a laugh. "I've driven past it enough times to know it's invisible. There aren't any landmarks to go off of."

"Well, I'm glad I'm not the only one that's missed it." I put my turn signal on and pulled over at the next dirt road. When the cars behind us cleared out, I spun around and went back, careful not to miss it a second time. I hate things that delay our arrival to an emergency. I know that one minute isn't enough to make a difference in most situations, but it's the principle.

The road went straight through the forest for over a mile. It was a real forest, too, not planted pines that would be logged out in a few years. I love places like this, places where people don't go. It's important for the rest of the animal kingdom to have their own space.

The trees ended, and the road was instead bracketed by wire fencing and pastures. To our left, a donkey and a mini horse stood beside each other, watching us. To our right, a beautiful Friesian horse cantered across the field, his jet-black coat gleaming in the sunshine. He tossed his head and whinnied.

"He looks excited to see us," I said. "I don't think that's our colic."

"He's not excited about us," Erica said, pointing ahead. "The colic is on the ground up there by the gate. Hurry up."

We don't normally speed on people's driveways, and it was certainly pointless now, since we were only a hundred yards away, but I pushed the gas down a bit more. There was a person standing by the fence, and another one running across the yard from the house. As we pulled to a stop, I could see that we were dealing with more than just a colic.

"He's got his front foot stuck in the fence," Erica said. "Don't get too close."

We hopped out of the vet truck just as the man running across the yard arrived. He was in his mid-fifties with white hair and a clear face, carrying a pair of wire cutters. He dropped to his knees at the fence. Erica joined him, grabbing the horse's hoof. The hoof and leg were covered in blood, making it impossible to see the extent of the injuries.

"I'll pull, you cut the wire," Erica said. "Hopefully he won't fight us."

I felt rather helpless, but there wasn't anything I could do at this point. Erica pulled on the horse's hoof, drawing it an inch further through the fence. His leg was narrower at this point, which allowed the guy to get the wire cutters on the strand of fence. The horse's white socks contrasted with the blood, making it look worse than it probably was. He was a bay, and had his legs been brown, like his back, the wound probably wouldn't look bad at all.

"Should I cut it in the middle or on the end?" he asked.

"Middle," Erica said. "As soon as you cut it, bend the ends away so he doesn't impale himself."

"Got it." He cut the fence just as the big Friesian came running by again. I was sure that the down horse would jerk his leg back, but he didn't.

"Duke is going to get us all killed," the woman muttered. "He's so stressed out about Wizzie that he doesn't know what to do with himself." She wrapped her hands around her elbows, nervously squeezing them as she watched.

With the wires bent away, the hole was twice as big. Blood dripped steadily to the ground, and one of the horse's heel bulbs looked to be torn away from the leg.

"Let's cut the top one while we're at it," Erica said. "He's got some skin hanging, and I'd rather not have him tear it off, if we can avoid it."

The man nodded and clipped the wire above the foot. He bent the ends away from the leg, and Erica pushed on the hoof, guiding it through the hole. The horse realized his foot was free, and jerkily climbed to his feet.

"Easy, buddy." Erica walked over to the gate and grabbed the halter hanging there. "Justin, can you grab my stethoscope and the thermometer?"

I jogged to the back of the truck and opened the liftgate. I handed her the stuff over the fence and stood poised to get whatever she asked for next. Carol held the lead rope for Erica, but the horse wasn't trying to go anywhere.

"Good morning," the man said, walking over to stand beside me. He stuck out his hand. "You caught us at a bad time, and I didn't get to introduce myself. I'm Sam, Carol's husband."

I shook his hand. "I'm Justin Long, Dr. Lacher's husband. Good to meet you. Sorry about the circumstances."

He laughed. "Well, it wasn't this bad when she called

earlier. Wizard just stuck his foot through the fence a few minutes ago. Before that, it was just a colic."

"Just a colic," Carol mimicked. "As if that's no big deal."

Erica pulled the stethoscope out of her ears. "He sounds pretty good. I'll palpate him in a minute, but I'm guessing he's just gassy. Can we walk him up to the barn? I'd like to get him on the wash rack and clean up his leg so we can see what's going on there."

"Sure thing." Carol tugged on the lead rope and clucked her tongue. "We need to get him away from Duke, anyway."

They got Wizard out of the pasture and started across the yard to the barn, walking under a beautiful old live oak tree. I climbed in the vet truck and pulled up the driveway, parking beside the open door of a long, low barn. The red paint had long since faded away, but it was still a charming scene, with wildflowers bedded on each side of the wide doorway, and a weathervane on the roof.

Sam hit the light switch as we walked inside, and a series of bright white LED light panels instantly dispelled the shadows. On the left were two wash bays with rubber mats on the concrete floor. It was fastidiously clean and organized, the way I wish ours was. Carol led Wizard into the first bay and slowly turned him around, clipping the cross ties to his halter once he was straightened out. I winced at the trail of blood droplets across the concrete. I didn't know which one of them was the OCD cleaner, but whoever it was, was going to be busy later. Erica grabbed the hose and handed it to me.

"You wash his foot while I palpate him. Keep it above the wounds and just let it run down over them."

"Got it." I turned the faucet on and began hosing down Wizard's leg. The water ran red across the mat to the floor drain, but it didn't take long to turn clear. The bleeding had mostly stopped already. He had scraped the hair off all the way around his pastern, and the skin was raw, but the only actual cut I could see was on his heel bulb.

Erica stepped away from the back of the horse, pulling the palpation sleeve off. "He's pretty gassed up, and he's got a small impaction. We'll get some drugs on board and pump him full of water and electrolytes, and he should be fine."

"What do you think about his leg?" Carol asked. She looked stressed, and Sam put his arm around her shoulders, squeezing her to him.

"One thing at a time, honey," Sam said, with a chuckle.

"No, no, it's okay," Erica said, squatting down to look at the leg. I turned off the hose. "He cut it pretty deep. We mainly worry about the tendon sheath and the coffin joint on these kinds of injuries. If those are both intact, it's just a matter of getting things healed up. If not, we'll have to do some serious antibiotics."

"Will that grow back together?" Carol asked.

"Oh, yeah, definitely," Erica said, probing the lacerated heel bulb. "The digital cushion is mostly elastic fibers and collagen. It's there to absorb impact, so it moves a lot, and that slows down the process. It'll heal slow, but it'll heal. Our biggest problem down the road will be keeping proud flesh from taking over."

I hung the hose back on the hook and followed Erica to the truck to get supplies. Having assisted in about a million colic emergencies, I knew exactly what my duties were. I pulled out the bucket, pump, hose, and the container of electrolytes, and grabbed the collapsible stool out of the back seat. Erica pulled up a few syringes of drugs and put them in the tray along with the bottle of lube, the clippers, and some bandaging material.

Back inside, we got to work. I unhooked the crossties and held the lead rope while Erica administered the shots. Once the sedation kicked in, Wizard's head would be drooping, and I didn't want the crossties supporting him. If he put too much weight on them, they might detach from the wall, and that would be a nasty surprise for everyone. We were also about to run an NG tube up his nose, and having them on crossties during that part is a bad plan. An ounce of prevention, as they say.

Wizard handled the tube better than most horses. He tossed his head and snorted once, but after that, he stood quietly. I scratched the white heart-shaped blaze on his forehead as Erica slid the tube up his nose. She blew into the end of the tube, confirming that it was in his stomach and not his lungs, and nodded at me.

"Okay, let's put some water in."

I draped the lead rope over his neck and sat down on the stool. Erica handed me the end of the tube, which I stuck on the pump. I glanced up at her. "Ready?"

"Yep."

I pumped the handle a few times, and when it was primed, I pumped it five times and stopped. The clear tube was filled with water, and I pulled it off the pump and lowered it down near the drain, creating a siphon. The water began flowing out, but soon stopped.

"Okay, let's put the salt in," Erica said.

"What were you checking for, there?" Sam asked.

"Reflux," Erica said. "Horses can't vomit, but if their system gets backed up, sometimes they need to. We want to make sure he doesn't already have a stomach full of water before we pump another three gallons in there."

Sam nodded. "Huh. So, they can't puke? That's a strange thing."

Erica shook her head with a chuckle. "There's a lot of bad design plans on horses. They stand on one finger, they're a hind-gut fermenter, they can't puke, and their primary reaction to everything bad is for their feet to fall off. Total design fail."

I dumped the salt mixture into the water bucket and began stirring it with the pump.

"This is a combination of Epsom salts, regular salt, light salt, and baking soda," Erica said. "One of the drugs I gave him is a smooth muscle relaxer, which will help his small intestine relax. The electrolyte solution will break down the impaction and push it through, rehydrate him, and make him drink more water."

"No mineral oil?" Sam asked. "That's what they always used when I was a kid."

Erica shook her head. "Nope, we don't use mineral oil anymore. It doesn't break down impactions, it doesn't hydrate the horse, and it doesn't replace the electrolytes they've lost. All it really does is make a mess when it comes out the other end."

"Was he dehydrated?" Sam asked.

"A bit, yeah. That's usually a factor when they have an impaction. Same as people, really. The more hydrated you are, the less likely you are to get constipated."

Sam shrugged. "Can't argue with that."

I slowly worked the pump handle up and down, occasionally pausing to stir the water. Wizard's head was down, and his hind end swayed back and forth. When the bucket was empty, I disconnected the tube from the pump and handed it to Erica. She blew into the end of the tube, forcing the remaining water into Wizard's stomach as she slowly pulled it out with her other hand. She handed it to me, and I coiled it up and stuck it in the bucket, setting it aside to be cleaned later.

"Okay," Erica said, squatting down. "Let's take a look at this foot."

With the blood washed away, the pastern looked less like a murder scene and more like raw meat, which wasn't much better. The fence wire had sliced about halfway through the heel bulb, which is a fleshy protrusion on the back of the foot, and the hair was gone where he had jerked it back and forth, trying to free himself. The skin was rubbed away in a few spots, and blood slowly seeped through in isolated droplets.

Erica patted Wizard on the cannon bone, and he lifted his foot off the ground with a sigh. She straddled his raised leg the way a farrier would, gripping the undamaged cannon bone with her knees so she could clearly see the back of his foot. With gentle fingers, she lifted the loose heel bulb and examined the area beneath it. I turned on the light from my phone to help her see it. A moment later, she set his foot back on the floor and stood up.

"Okay. It doesn't look too bad from here, but these injuries can be deceiving. We need to make sure he didn't compromise the tendon sheath or the joint inside there. Once we make that determination, we can make a plan."

"How can you tell that?" Sam asked. "Can you see it on an x-ray or something?"

Erica shook her head. "No, we inject sterile fluid in one end, and see if it comes out the other. We can't rely on visuals for something like this, because bacteria can get in some pretty tiny holes that we'd never see. Infection is the big concern. Joints just don't handle infections very well."

I followed Erica out to the truck to get the needed supplies.

I'd helped with a joint perfusion before, but never a tendon sheath. In a weird way, I was excited to be learning something new. Erica handed me the tray and began piling things into it.

"Remind me that we need to go restock on small fluids when we get done here," she said.

I nodded. "I'll do my best." If my hands hadn't been full, I would've put a reminder in my phone. Remembering something like that through this emergency was a long shot, and I knew better than to rely on my memory.

When we got back in the barn, Erica set me to scrubbing Wizard's leg.

"Start in the center with a chlorahex gauze, and go in circles, bigger and bigger. Then do the same thing with the alcohol gauze. Then do it again, over and over. It'll take a while. When I tell you, move down here and scrub this spot, too." She pointed to a spot further down.

I nodded and starting scrubbing. At first it was easy. The chlorahex gauze was slippery and turned into light green soap suds as I scrubbed. Then the alcohol gauze would rinse off the soap. The gauze would come away dirty, but each one was progressively less dirty. However, after about two minutes of this, my fingers started getting sore. I glanced at Erica, hoping she would call it good, but she was busy injecting drugs into one of the bags of fluids. After three minutes, my whole hand started cramping. Who knew cleaning a pastern could be so painful? The gauze was coming away clean, and I showed it to Erica.

"Is that good?" I asked hopefully.

"I think so," Erica said. "Go ahead and scrub the other spot."

I switched hands and went through the whole process of

pain and cramping all over again. Carol and Sam had brought over lawn chairs so they could sit and watch us, and I didn't want to complain in front of them, but I didn't think I could go on much longer. The gauze began coming away clean at last, and Erica finally gave me the reprieve I so desperately needed.

"Okay, that's good."

I held back a gasp of relief as I dropped the final alcohol gauze in the pile that had accumulated. I'm a little OCD, so the green chlorohex gauze was heaped on the left, and the alcohol gauze was piled on the right. I'll admit it. Sometimes I'm weird, but I like having a neat workspace. Erica doesn't suffer from this at all, but I don't hold it against her. Much.

She handed me the fluid bag to hold and went over the spot I'd cleaned one more time with an alcohol gauze wipe, then tossed it on the floor. Not in my nice pile, either. I glared at her, but she was busy poking a needle into Wizard's leg and didn't notice.

"Okay, squeeze the bag," she said, squatting down further to watch his leg. "Not too hard, just keep steady pressure on it."

My hands had recovered some of their strength, and the size of the bag of fluids made it reasonably manageable. I rolled the end of the bag down to the water level, then wrapped both hands around it and squeezed it like a rubber ball. Nothing happened, but I held the pressure. We stayed like that for about a minute.

"Okay, that looks good."

I released the pressure on the bag. Wizard just stood there, and I scratched his forehead while Erica pulled the needle out. "Halfway there, buddy, just hang in there."

Erica did a final cleaning on the injection site for the coffin joint, tossed the gauze on the floor away from my nice, neat pile, then put a fresh needle on the line. "Okay, here we go."

She got her spot, then leaned away as she inserted the needle. Wizard stood like a stone, and I silently thanked him for not kicking Erica. It's always scary when she pokes a needle into a joint, as you never know how the horse will react. Sedated or not, it's dangerous every time.

We repeated the process from before, and once again, there was no leakage. The joint was intact.

"Two and oh," Erica said, pulling the needle out of his joint. "You dodged a mighty big bullet on this one, kiddo." She patted his neck.

"Oh, thank you, Jesus!" Carol sprang to her feet and wrapped her arms around Wizard's neck. "Oh, that's what I wanted to hear."

"Where does that leave us?" Sam asked. He stood by his chair, and some of the lines had smoothed out of his face.

"We're going to bandage it for now," Erica said. "It's going to drain a lot at first, so we'll let that happen. On Monday, I'll come back out and put a cast on it to minimize the movement. It'll take some time, but it looks like he'll be okay."

Carol turned and hugged Sam, pressing her face into his chest. He stroked her hair, smiling apologetically to us over the top of her head. I smiled back with a shrug. It wasn't as if he needed to explain anything. For us, animals are family.

I handed supplies to Erica as she bandaged Wizard's leg. He stood quietly, his lower lip hanging loose in the way that all sedated horses have, which always makes me laugh. I was disappointed that I wouldn't be there to help her put the cast on the following week. It's probably not that exciting to watch, but I like being there to see everything that happens. It's all very interesting to be a part of, especially when I think about where veterinary medicine was at a hundred years ago. We've come a long way.

There was a nagging question in the back of my mind that was bothering me as we packed up to leave. I waited until we were driving away to ask Erica about it. She was staring out the window at the woods, and I hesitated, unsure of why I was even asking her. There wasn't an answer, after all.

"When we got here, I missed the turn," I said.

She turned to look at me. "Yeah?"

I glanced at her, then returned my eyes to the road, trying to choose my words. "I can't help but wonder, if I hadn't missed the turn, if we would have gotten there before Wizard stuck his foot through the fence. Maybe it wouldn't have happened."

She was silent for a moment, and I mistook that for an agreement with my thoughts. When she spoke, I realized that wasn't the case at all.

"Justin, sometimes I want to reach inside your head and grab that thing that makes you blame yourself for everything and yank it out."

I shot her a sideways glance, surprised by the intensity in her voice. She wasn't finished.

"There's a hundred things that could have delayed us by a minute or two. A red light. A car turning in front of us. I might have run back in the house to grab the computer or use the bathroom before we left. So, no, you don't get to beat yourself up for what happened. Wizard was in pain, and he stuck his foot through the fence while he was rolling around. That's the whole thing. You weren't part of any of that. Do you understand what I'm saying?"

I stopped the truck, put it in park, and leaned over, wrapping my arms around her. "Thank you," I whispered. "That's why you're the one."

She ruffled my hair as I put the truck back in gear. We held hands in a companionable silence most of the way home. I don't know what she was thinking about, but I was going over all the ways that Erica has made me a better person. Not allowing me to beat myself up for things is a big one, but it's just one item on a long list.

Chapter 18

Stuck in a Loop

Not all horse emergencies involve illness or injury. Sometimes a horse just gets itself in a bad situation, and we're there to get it out the safest way possible. I've been witness to several of these situations, and they're always interesting. They can be terrifying as well, as there's usually a risk of something horrible happening.

We were on our way back home from a gas colic one Sunday morning. It was a beautiful spring day, and I was making a mental list of all the things I wanted to get done outside while the weather was nice. The compost bin was due to be shoveled out, and I wanted to put the compost on the flower beds and around the young trees. That was my plan, but the Universe had other plans.

"Hello, Dr. Lacher."

We were just south of High Springs, Florida, and I took my foot off the gas pedal and pulled over on the shoulder. At least half of our clients were north of here, and if we were going to be turning around, I didn't want to keep going south.

"Does he seem to be in pain?" Erica asked.

That wasn't one of her normal questions.

"Okay. Let's not do anything to stress him out. We're literally right up the road, so just sit tight until we get there."

I've listened to a lot of emergency phone calls, and I can almost always figure out what the situation is before Erica hangs up. This wasn't one of those times. She pointed down the road as she wrapped up the call, and I pulled back onto the road.

"What's going on?" I asked.

"That was Linda Rodriguez. She's right up here on the left, just before the power lines. Bogie's stuck in the hay ring. Her neighbor came over to help, but he can't do it by himself."

"Didn't she just have shoulder surgery?" I asked. "I saw something about it on Facebook a few weeks ago." I slowed down and put my turn signal on. At less than a minute, this was going to be a record response time to an emergency.

"Yeah, she said she can't do much to help Dale."

The house was an older single-level ranch style with red brick and a white shingle roof. I'd been here once before for a regular vaccine appointment when I was filling in for one of the techs, and I remembered that it was a good idea to turn around at the house and back down to the barn. The dirt driveway was lined with flowers, so you either had to back in or back out. I opted to back in.

The barn wasn't really a barn, or at least not in the classic sense. The low metal roof covered a stall on each side up front, and a wooden wall separated the two stalls from an open covered area on the back side. Linda stood beside the barn and waved us over as we got out of the truck.

"I can't believe you got here so fast," she called out. "He's right around here."

I opened the gate and followed Erica through, closing it behind me. Linda was dressed for church in a simple blue dress, her silver hair in a neat bun, and I nearly laughed to see her standing in the paddock in high heels. That's horse people for you.

We rounded the corner, and my heart skipped a beat. Bogie, an older Appaloosa gelding, lay on his side in a giant mess of hay that used to be a round roll. His front left leg was stuck between the rails of a metal hay ring, the kind that you often see used with cattle. The ring was bent out of shape, and he had clearly been struggling violently to extricate himself from it. His back legs were straddling one of the posts that supported the roof. He was definitely in a pickle.

Dale, an overweight middle-aged man with thinning salt and pepper hair, was bent over one side of the ring, removing screws from the upper rail. Bogie whinnied as we came into view, and kicked out with his free foot, striking the hay ring. Dale jumped back.

"Oh, boy," Erica said. "Bogie, what have you done to yourself?"

He lifted his head up for a moment, then let it fall back with a sigh. Sweat covered his neck and flanks, and the ground beneath him was churned up from his flailing hooves.

"I'm trying to take the top rail off the ring," Dale said. "Some of the screw are bent, though, so I think we're gonna have to cut it apart. He's got it all bent up around his leg. What do you think, doc?"

He was looking at me as he said this, and I pointed at Erica with a grin. "She's the doc. I just drive the truck and carry the heavy stuff."

"We're going to have to sedate him," Erica said. "I don't want him to rip his leg off when we start moving things around. Do we know how long he's been here?"

Linda shrugged. "He started raising a racket about 7:45, right before I came out to feed, and that's been nearly an hour, now. Dale came right over, but we haven't been able to get the ring moved. I just had rotator cuff surgery, so I can't do much to help him."

Erica nodded. "Okay. We're going to sedate him pretty heavily. Once he's knocked out, I think the three of us can get the ring pulled off. We'll have to drag him out away from the pole and flip him over. His down-side is probably numb by now from laying on it so long."

"It might help if we get some of this hay out of the way," Dale said. "That was part of my problem, the hay kept me from being able to move the ring very far."

"Okay," Erica said. "Let's get him knocked out before we do anything else. I don't want him to move at all, if we can avoid it."

Dale stepped over beside Linda, stretching his back, and I followed Erica to the truck to get the drugs and supplies. While she pulled up the sedative, I grabbed a towel to put under Bogie's head to protect his eye. This was a prime opportunity for an eye injury, and we wanted to avoid that if possible. Erica handed me the rope from the top of the vet box, and we went back to the barn.

I stopped beside Linda and Dale, and we watched as Erica crouched down, slowly reaching out to put a hand on Bogie's neck. She was behind him, so it wasn't too dangerous for her, but he could still injure himself significantly if he panicked and tried to stand up. Horses aren't any better at being vulnerable than people are, and being stuck flat on your back is scary when people are moving around you and stabbing you with things. I held my breath as she inched closer. She rubbed his neck, talking softly to him as she slowly got into a position where she could give him the shot. At last, she slid the needle into the big vein in his neck, pressing the plunger down. Bogie lay still, breathing heavily.

It took a few minutes for the drugs to take effect. Since he was already on the ground, a lot of the usual steps in the process didn't happen. When a horse is sedated while standing, there's a lot of swaying and leg wobbling that takes place as they fight the loss of muscle control. That's followed by a controlled fall, where Erica uses the halter to push them back on their haunches, and then over to one side, holding their head so it doesn't slam into the ground. This is a system employed to minimize the risk of a broken leg or an eye injury.

Bogie's breathing eventually slowed, and his body relaxed. We gave him another minute, then Erica grabbed the towel from me and lifted Bogie's head, sliding the towel under his face and wrapping it around to cover both eyes. He was out cold, and Erica put us to work.

"Alright, let's get that hay out of there. Don't throw it on the far side, because we'll need the maneuvering space to slide the ring over."

"Do you want me to get my Sawzall?" Dale asked. "I can just cut it right off there."

Erica shook her head. "No, we can't do that. He's sedated, but he's still totally capable of freaking out and breaking his leg. I don't even want to hacksaw it if we don't have to. I think we can stand the ring up on its side and slide it over once we get the hay out of the way."

"Got it," Dale said. "How long do we have before the drugs wear off?"

"Not long," Erica said. "Twenty minutes or so. I can give him more if we need to, but we'll start with that. I need him to be able to stand up once we get him out of here so I can see how bad he hurt himself."

We started throwing handfuls of hay over to one side. There was a lot of it, but once we got the loose stuff moved, we were able to do the rest of it in big clumps. It was heavy and awkward, but with three of us, we managed it. The last chunk was the worst. It was the center of the roll, and still pretty compressed. Without having the wrapper around it, the hay just unraveled in our hands. The three of us formed a circle around it, pushing in towards each other as we lifted. We staggered to the hay ring, trying to position ourselves to toss it over the side.

"Don't drop it on the rail," Erica said. "We'll heave it over on three. Ready?"

We nodded and counted together. "One, two, three."

With a mighty shove, the core of the bale spilled over the ring and down the other side of the pile, falling apart as it rolled. I brushed my hands on my pants, trying to catch my breath. There was still a lot of hay on the ground, but not enough to impede our mission.

"Okay," Erica said, stepping out of the ring. "Now the fun part."

I lifted one side of the hay ring experimentally, trying to gauge its weight. It was heavier than I expected.

"We need to lift this side up," Erica said, pointing to the edge opposite of Bogie's leg. "If we can get it up to about forty-five degrees, that ought to let his leg slide out. Then we just have to slide it that way."

"If you'll help us get it off the ground, I think we can probably manage it while you guide his leg," I said. I wasn't sure if Dale and I could manage it or not, but it seemed like a good place to start.

"Okay." She stepped over beside me. "Are we ready?"

Dale and I lined up with each other on the sides and grabbed the lower rail. Erica stood between us, poised to lift.

"Here we go," Dale grunted.

At first, I thought the hay ring weighed a thousand pounds. When it broke free from the dirt, I realized it wasn't that bad after all, it had just been tromped down in the mud the last time it rained. We angled it up until the bent rails around Bogie's leg were horizontal. I shuffled around until I was holding the lower rail on my shoulder as Erica let go and went around to Bogie. Dale followed my lead.

"Let's try to slide it over," Erica said. "Nice and easy. If he moves his leg, we're just going to freeze in place."

"Watch the roof," I said. "We don't want to catch that rafter."

Dale glanced up and nodded. "Got it."

Erica lifted the back end with one hand and held Bogie's leg up with the other. It was awkward, but we managed to scoot it out a few inches before we got hung up on a dirt clod. Dale repositioned himself to get better leverage and we did it again. The ring scraped across the ground, dragging hay and dirt with it. The upper rail bounced and clanged with the movement, the few remaining screws keeping it from crashing down. I prayed that they wouldn't break and let it fall on us.

The only thing left inside the ring was Bogie's hoof. Erica pushed the rail with her hip as we strained to pull it the last few inches. The bent pipes made it a tight squeeze, but at last his foot was free. Dale and I made eye contact, and slowly lowered the hay ring to the ground. As hard as we had worked, it felt like we must have moved it at least ten feet, but it was really closer to two feet. Einstein's theory of relativity was hard at work.

Freeing his leg was a giant step forward, but we were far from finished. We still had to drag him away from the post that his rear legs were straddling. That wasn't going to be easy.

"Okay, how are we going to do this?" I asked.

Erica pointed to the rope I had dropped beside the tray. "First, we'll drag him out a bit, then we're going to flip him over. That will get him off the pole and let some blood start flowing through his muscles again. He's going to have a serious case of the tingles."

I shuddered at the thought. There are few sensations that I hate worse than my foot waking up, and I couldn't imagine how bad it would be for my whole leg to be asleep.

Erica grabbed the rope and tied one end around Bogie's rear leg, the one closest to the ground, then moved up to his head. "Justin, you get his tail. Dale, you grab his mane, right here beside me. We're going to pull him out just a bit at a time."

"Why can't we just pull him by the leg?" Dale asked. "I'm not arguing, just curious, since you already got the rope on it."

"We don't want to damage his joints. We could hyper-extend his hock if we pulled it this way while he's sedated."

"Ahh, I see," Dale said. "He can't push against it."

"Right." We all got a good hold, and Erica counted us down. "Three, two, one, go."

We heaved and strained, and Bogie slid forward a few inches. Linda bent down and straightened the towel over his eyes. We tugged a second time, and he came out a few more inches. We stood up to rest our backs for a second and get a better grip.

"One more time ought to do it," Erica said. "Then we'll roll him over. That'll have him pointing in the right direction."

Bogie snorted as we get a fresh hold on him. "The sedation's wearing off," Erica said. "Let's get this done."

With one last mighty effort, we slid Bogie out nearly six inches. I leaned back, silently apologizing to my back for treating it this way. Erica grabbed the rope and waved us out of the way.

She drew the slack out of the rope, pulling his lower leg up off the ground. I've seen her do this many times, but it's always a sight to see. She positioned herself near his shoulder, so that the rope was running diagonal across his torso. Wrapping the rope around her waist, she backed up slowly. His hindquarters raised up, pulling his front end up with them. She inched back further, keeping a steady tension on the rope. All four of his legs were in the air now. His back legs passed the vertical point, and gravity began to help her. As his rear legs came down, his upper body and head flopped over.

"Ta-da!" I sang out. Linda clapped and Dale chuckled, shaking his head.

"I've never seen that done," he said. "That's a pretty good trick."

"You can do it with cast horses that aren't totally knocked

out, too," Erica said. "The hard part is getting the rope back off their foot."

She walked around behind Bogie and carefully untied the knot. "You have to be careful how you tie it, too. You don't want it cinching down on the leg when you pull."

"Makes sense," Dale said. He turned to Linda. "Well, it looks like things are under control here. I'm gonna head back over to the house and finish morning chores. Let me know if you need anything."

Linda gave him a brief hug. "Thank you so much for coming over. I really appreciate it."

"Any time, you know that. I'll give you a call this afternoon and we'll figure out what to do about the hay ring and all that."

As Dale walked away, Erica put a halter on Bogie, draping the lead rope over his neck so it wouldn't get wrapped around his legs when he started moving around. I took the rope and the used needles to the truck while we waited for Bogie to wake up and brought the x-ray machine over. We had to run the extension cord from the other side of the barn, and it just reached. By the time I had it up and running, Bogie was sitting up, looking around blankly.

"I think he's confused about how he got from there to here," I chuckled.

"I think he's dealing with some overwhelming tingling all down his right side," Erica said. Somehow, I'd forgotten about that part. I cringed again, imagining the sensation.

After a few minutes of sitting sternal, he lunged forward. His back legs kicked at the ground, but he couldn't get enough purchase to stand up. He fell back, his head flopping to the ground.

"Easy, buddy," Erica said, reaching out to grasp the lead rope. "There's no rush. Just hang out until you're ready."

Bogie lay flat for a few minutes, breathing heavily. His efforts had moved him another foot away from the post behind him, so that was good. There was nothing else to impede him now but the waning sedatives in his system. We waited quietly as he gathered his strength.

I looked over at the wrecked hay ring and the remains of the round roll. It looked like a tornado had come through here. I didn't envy Dale the task of returning all this to some semblance of order. At the same time, it occurred to me how fortunate Linda was to have someone like Dale to help her out. Taking care of a horse by yourself is manageable most of the time, but when you're injured, something like this would be impossible.

With a great intake of air, Bogie sat up again, and immediately lunged to his feet. Erica took a quick step back as he gained his equilibrium. He weaved around for a few minutes, lifting one foot, then another. Erica led him forward a few steps, watching carefully as he placed his weight on the front left leg. He didn't seem to mind using it, and beside me, Linda let out a sigh of relief.

"Well, thank God it isn't broken."

"Nope, it doesn't seem to be," Erica agreed. "We'll take a few images and make sure there's nothing serious going on inside, but he looks surprisingly good." She led him over to the other side of the barn where the x-ray machine was set up. After donning the lead vests, Linda held the lead rope, I held the plate, and Erica shot the pictures. It didn't take long.

"He's probably going to be sore for a day or two, but he managed to avoid hurting himself seriously." Erica took the halter off Bogie and patted his neck. "We'll keep him on some anti-inflammatory drugs for a few days, but I think he's going to be just fine."

I began packing up the x-ray machine as Erica and Linda talked. Sometimes things work out this way, where it seems really bad in the beginning, and everything turns out alright in the end. Sometimes it goes the other way, where things don't seem too bad, but then everything goes wrong. You just never know with horses.

When we got home, I looked at the compost bin and thought about my earlier plans to shovel it out. After wrestling with the hay ring and dragging Bogie around, I wasn't sure if my back was up for it or not. I decided to at least get started on it. When you're on call, having time later to get stuff done isn't a guarantee. You gotta do what you can while you have the opportunity. That's a good philosophy for all things in life, really. Seize the moment, right?

Chapter 19

THE SHARP TONGUE

IT WAS 8:00 PM ON A THURSDAY NIGHT, and we had just finished up the monthly seminar that we host at our veterinary clinic. People were milling around, talking to friends, and asking questions of the doctors. I had a table set up next to the PA system so that I could display my sci-fi book series and still run the sound system and record the seminar. A few people came over to talk about books, including a young girl of eleven or twelve. When she got to the front of the line, I sat down so we could talk eye to eye.

"Hi there," I said with a grin. "Are you a sci-fi fan?"

She nodded, an earnest expression on her face. "I read all kinds of books. What're yours about?"

Most times, I don't have much interaction with kids, and it's always difficult to figure out how to appropriately speak to their comprehension level. I didn't want to talk down to her, but I also didn't want to confuse her. I decided to speak as if she were an adult. That's how I preferred for people to talk to me when I was that age, and if she was a reader, she probably had a pretty good vocabulary.

"This series is about multiple dimensions of reality. There's a company that has a portal system to travel between the different worlds, and they use it to enslave people in some dimensions and make them work in mines and things like that, then they sell the products in other dimensions. The hero is a computer guy who works for this company and figures out what they're doing. He goes on the warpath to try and stop them. It's an underdog story, because it's just him and his best friend against a massive conglomerate."

She picked up a copy of *Genesis Dimension* and read the flap. I sat in silence, letting her read. When she finished, she looked over the other books in the series, then turned her serious eyes back to me. "How much are they?"

I gave her the price.

"I'll be right back." She turned away, flipping her pale blonde braid over her shoulder.

The seminar video had finished loading to YouTube, so I shut down the computer and started putting microphones away and rolling up cables. When I turned back to the table, the girl was there, showing her mother the books.

"Is there anything inappropriate in them?" her mother asked, gesturing at the table.

"There's some swearing," I said. "Not a ton, but it's probably PG-13. There's no romance of any kind, nothing like that."

There was a whispered argument between them, and I tried to keep the smile off my face. It was the first time I had ever seen someone really want my book, and it felt great. I decided that if her mom wasn't willing to spend the money on one, I'd give it to her for free. A moment later, I learned that I was misunderstanding the situation slightly. The woman pulled some cash out of her pocket and handed it to her daughter, then walked back over to the group of people she'd been talking to.

"I'd like a copy of *Genesis Dimension*," the girl said. "I wanted the whole series, but my mom says I have to read the first book first and see if I like it."

I sat back down and grabbed my pen. "That's pretty good advice. If you do like it, you can get the second book at the next seminar, how about that?"

She rolled her eyes. "I'll probably finish the whole book this weekend, and then I'll have to wait a month to get the next one."

I laughed. "I know what you mean. But you can get the rest of the books on Amazon, you don't have to wait until you come back here again. What's your name?"

"Ellie." Her face lit up at the news.

"Alright, Ellie," I said, signing the book to her with a flourish. "Here you go. Make sure you grab a bookmark."

"Thanks!" She opened the book and began reading immediately as she drifted over near her mother.

As the crowd cleared out, I took the PA system apart and loaded it back in the truck. The books and table went next, and the whole team pitched in to get the chairs loaded in the back end. We had just finished when the emergency phone line rang.

"Hello, Dr. Lacher."

Everyone paused and waited to see what was going on.

"No worries. Bring her in, we're all still here." She hung up the phone. "Cindy Breman's bringing The Dude in. Apparently, he's trying to eat, but food is just falling right back out of his mouth with a lot of saliva, and he was fine this morning."

Amy glanced around. "Wasn't she just here, like ten minutes ago?"

Dr. Allison laughed. "Right? I just saw her daughter buy one of Justin's books. How could they have an emergency already?"

Erica shrugged. "They live right down the road. She said she dumped feed as soon as she got home, and he's acting really weird. It's probably an infected tooth."

"I'll pull up his records and see when we did his last dental," Amy said. "I swear it was less than six months ago."

"I'll get the dental gear out," Cassie volunteered.

I hopped in my truck and pulled it around the front of the clinic so Cindy and The Dude could get into the stocks area, where I had been set up during the seminar. It was getting late, but no one on the staff was leaving. I'm always impressed with their desire to be involved in everything. Some of them were working on getting into veterinary school, so every emergency they could see was an opportunity to gain knowledge and experience. For everyone else, it was just love of horses, and the excitement of the whole thing.

We didn't have to wait long. Ten minutes after the phone call, a pair of headlights swung through the front gate, and a truck and horse trailer pulled around back. I couldn't help but notice that Ellie was still carrying her new book as they led the horse in.

"Welcome back!" Cassie called, waving them in. "Bring him right on up here, and we'll get him in the stocks."

"It's like we were just here," Cindy said with a wry grin. "I think The Dude was mad that we didn't bring him on the first trip."

Once the horse was in the stocks, Erica pulled his lips apart and took a sniff in his mouth. "It doesn't stink. Let's get the speculum on him and take a look inside."

The team went to work, and I stepped over to the side with Cindy and Ellie.

"Why did she smell his breath?" Ellie asked.

"That's one way of finding out if they have an infected tooth," I said. "It stinks really bad when they have an infection."

With the speculum holding his mouth open, Erica used a giant syringe to squirt water into his mouth. Cassie held a bucket underneath his head to catch the water as it ran back out. They rinsed his mouth repeatedly until all the food was out, then Erica turned on her headlamp and looked inside.

After her initial inspection, she grabbed the long-handled mirror and slid it into his mouth, turning it this way and that. She switched sides and repeated the process, and finally put the mirror back on the table.

"Hhmmm." She stepped back and switched the light off. "I don't see anything wrong with his teeth on the surface. Let's grab the x-ray and see if he's got a broken tooth or something."

With three doctors and three techs on hand, as well as the office crew, it only took a minute to get everything set up. Everyone crowded around the screen as the images of The Dude's mouth started showing up.

"I can't see anything wrong," Dr. Russel said. "His roots look great, no cracks in the teeth, nothing."

"What's that?" Dr. Allison asked, pointing at the screen.

"That tiny line there in the middle. It almost looks like he has something in his tongue."

Erica blew up the image, and they stared at it for a moment. As one, they turned to the horse. They put the speculum back in place, and Erica turned her headlamp back on. They all peered into his mouth. After glancing back at the x-ray to confirm the location, Erica grabbed his tongue and pulled it over so they could see the side of it.

"There's a bit of a red spot there," Dr. Allison said. She grabbed the mirror and used it as a pointer.

"Yep, I see that," Dr. Russel agreed. "But what could he have in his tongue that would show up on the x-ray? It has to be metal, right?"

Erica nodded. "Yeah, but it's tiny, like a needle."

Beside me, Cindy slowly turned to stare at Ellie, her hands going to her hips. The expression on her face made me take a step backwards.

"Were you sewing in the barn?"

Ellie's face turned flaming red.

"You were headed to the barn with your sewing stuff earlier, and I told you not to take it out there. Did you do it anyway?"

Ellie nodded ever so slightly. I wanted to crawl under a rock, and I wasn't even the one in trouble. Having spent a large part of my childhood in trouble, I knew exactly how she felt.

"I didn't mean to lose it," she whispered.

I thought Cindy's head might explode, but she managed to keep her voice even. "What did you lose, Ellie?"

Tears rolled down Ellie's cheeks at last, and I could barely understand her. "A n-ne-needle."

"You lost a needle, and The Dude managed to get it stuck in his tongue," Cindy said.

The words fell out of my mouth before I could stop them. "Talk about a needle in a haystack." I cringed, but Cindy managed a lopsided grin.

"What are the odds?" She shook her head and turned to the doctors. "So, it seems that it probably is a needle. I guess we're learning lessons the hard way today." She glared at Ellie.

"Alrighty, then. Let's get it out of there." Erica nodded to Dr. Allison. "You spotted it, it's all yours."

Dr. Allison nodded. "Let's get him some sedation. This might be a tough extraction."

While The Dude was processing the drugs, Dr. Allison studied the x-ray, and Cassie used a towel to dry off his tongue. Ellie stood behind her mother, biting her lip. I felt bad for her. This was a hard way to learn a lesson.

I couldn't see a thing when they got to work. Terry held The Dude's head on her shoulder, Cassie held his tongue with a towel, and Dr. Allison probed the area, trying to find the needle and get a grip on it. It took nearly fifteen minutes, which seemed like an eternity, but at last, she held the forceps up in the air.

"I give you the proverbial needle," she announced.

Everyone cheered. Well, not everyone. Ellie looked like she'd rather be anywhere else on the planet. Cindy accepted the freshly cleaned needle from Cassie and showed it to Ellie. "This is why we don't take sharp things to the barn. Do you understand now?"

Ellie nodded miserably. "Yes, Mom."

I patted her on the back as they headed inside to take care of the paperwork. It's hard being a kid. At least she had a new book to escape into. In a week, this would all be a distant memory for her. The Dude was going to be fine, too, and all's well that ends well, right?

Chapter 20

WILD CHILD

I'VE GOTTEN PRETTY GOOD at not hearing the phone ring over the years, at least when I'm in a dead sleep, but the sound of Erica's voice always wakes me up. It usually happens that I'm in the middle of a dream, and what she's saying doesn't mesh at all with what I was dreaming about, which can lead to some confusion on my part. This was one of those nights.

As I struggled to wake up and make sense of what was going on, a cat jumped on my stomach. That woke me right up. Erica had turned on the lamp on her nightstand and was sitting on the edge of the bed.

"Yep, it sounds like it needs to be seen," she was saying. "Have we been out to your farm before?"

I pushed the cat off my bladder and rolled over with a groan. According to the alarm clock, I had only been in bed for an hour. No wonder I was so sleepy.

"Let me get an address," Erica said. She scribbled it down on a notepad. "Okay, we're about forty-five minutes away. We'll be there as soon as we can. If you can catch her, go ahead and start hosing the wound."

Part of being who I am means I do a lot of math problems in my head. I know, it's weird, but it's how I'm wired. I started doing some quick calculations. If it was a forty-five-minute drive each way, and we were probably going to be there for close to an hour, it was going to be 2:00 am before we made it back to bed. I sat up and rubbed my face as Erica hung up the phone.

"Laceration?" I asked.

"Yep, on a horse that hasn't been handled in two years." Erica got up and began getting dressed. "The horses belonged to their daughter, but she got killed in a car wreck a few years ago, so they just run free in a pasture now."

"How did they even know one got hurt?" I asked.

"I guess it screamed enough to get their attention. I didn't ask."

I followed her out to the porch and slipped my shoes on. Despite the late hour, it was still near eighty degrees and quite humid. That's typical for Florida, but it still catches me off guard when my glasses fog up the instant I step out the door.

We rode in silence most of the way. The radio was on low, but our focus was on the road. The entire route was on small country roads, and the glow of eyeballs in the dark areas just off the pavement made it impossible to think about much of anything other than not running over any wildlife. The silence was broken only by an occasional warning.

"Deer on the right."

"Got it."

At last we found the mailbox we were looking for, and turned onto a long, winding dirt road. After a few minutes of creeping through a dense, dark forest, the trees fell away, revealing an old farmhouse. In the headlights, I could just make out the shape of a low building behind it. As we pulled around the side of the house, Erica pointed to a flashlight waving back and forth in the pasture to the right.

"Looks like they haven't caught her yet," she said.

"Oh, boy." I pulled up next to the gate and parked, leaving the headlights on bright so we could see what we were doing. An elderly woman with a walker stepped out of the small barn on the other side of the fence and began to slowly make her way over.

"That must be Emma," Erica said. "Let me run over there and talk to her. She's going to hurt herself trying to run around out here in the dark. You go see if you can find the halter in the back. I think it's underneath the vet box."

While she went to talk to the horse owner, I opened the back end and started hunting for the halter. It wasn't under the vet box, of course. Nothing is ever that easy in the middle of the night when there's an injured horse running around a giant field. I pulled the headlamp out and put it on. It was much brighter than my phone, and not having to hold something made digging around a lot easier.

Most things are easy to find in the vet truck. It's an SUV, and the back end is filled with a big metal box with drawers that slide out nearly all the way. We keep things very organized so that no matter who the technician is, or which doctor they're with, they can find what they need right away. The exceptions to the rule are things that are bulky, like the big rolls of cotton batting, or seldom-used things like the halter. These items get shoved in the space beside the box, or in the gap underneath it, or on top with the printer. I finally located the halter at the very bottom of the stack of things crammed in the left side and met Erica at the gate.

"Can you please not shine the headlamp in my eyes?" Erica asked.

"Shit." I fumbled for the switch on the back of the headband. "I'm sorry. I wasn't thinking."

"I'm just trying to preserve my night vision. It looks like I'm going to need it." She turned to look out into the darkness beyond the barn. "So, here's the situation. There are three horses out there. We're looking for a black mare with a big gash on her shoulder. She's out at the round bale, but Herb hasn't been able to catch her."

"And he's been trying for an hour," I said with a chuckle. "This sounds like a good time."

"Yeah, well, he's in his seventies, and he probably doesn't get around much better than his wife," Erica said. "Run back to the truck and get a handful of treats and the clicker. We're going to do this the easy way."

I returned a moment later with my pockets stuffed full of treats and handed Erica the clicker. We transferred some of the treats to her pocket before heading out into the pasture, and I gave her the headlamp.

"Hey, pony," Erica called out into the darkness. "Hey, girl." She shut the headlamp off as we neared the hay bale.

"She's on the other side of the round roll," the man said, shining his light at us. "I almost had a hand on her once, but she's spooky."

"Okay, that's fine," Erica said. "I'm just letting her know we're here. We're going to come up from the other side and try to talk her down, if you want to just stay on this side."

I stayed with Erica as she circled around the right side of the hay bale, away from Herb on the other side. The moon was bright, which helped my eyes adjust to the darkness. As we came closer, I could see the dark shape of a horse standing behind the hay.

"Stay back here," Erica said quietly. She took the halter from me and edged closer to the horse, talking softly to her. I stopped and watched. I couldn't hear what she was saying, but within a minute I heard the distinct sound of the clicker as she gave the horse a treat. She patted the horse on the neck. They did this a few more times before Erica carefully slipped the lead rope around the horse's neck. The horse raised her head and snorted, but Erica stayed right with her, talking calmly. When the horse's head dropped back down, the clicker clicked again, and a moment later the halter was on.

"I don't reckon I've ever seen somebody that slick with a horse before," the old man said.

Erica laughed. "You just have to speak their language." She looked away from the horse, turned her headlamp on, and carefully turned back to inspect the wound. I stepped around them so I could see better.

A huge flap of bloody skin hung off the shoulder, revealing a wide red triangle of muscle. The black hair absorbed the light, but the blood trickling down her leg reflected it in small diamonds all the way down to her hoof. Flies buzzed around the wound, crawling across the wet skin below it. Erica carefully lifted the hanging flap of skin and looked beneath it before stepping back.

"Okay, it doesn't look like she damaged the muscle," she said. "I know it looks terrible, but it's not near as bad as it looks. Let's get her over to the barn and we'll get her stitched up."

"She's a bit squirrelly," Herb said. "She ain't used to being told what to do."

"We'll take it easy," Erica said. "Once we get some drugs into her, she'll be fine."

I kept my distance from them as we walked back, just to be on the safe side, but we arrived at the barn without incident. We stopped out front, and Erica handed me the lead rope and a water hose.

"Run this over the wound until I get back."

"Directly on the wound?" I asked.

"Right above it, so it runs down over everything." She turned on the faucet, and a slow stream of water came out. "Just like that. I'll be right back."

Erica disappeared into the darkness, and Herb turned his flashlight on the horse so I could see. It wasn't near as bright as Erica's headlamp, and the hanging flap of skin was nearly invisible in the feeble yellow glow. The horse shifted uncomfortably, trying to get away from the water hose.

"What's her name?" I asked.

"Toots," Emma said. "She's Toots, and her sister is Boots."

"Easy, Toots," I said, putting a hand on her neck. I couldn't help but smile at the name. "Easy, girl. We're going to get you fixed up. Just hang in there."

I'm not a skilled horse handler like Erica is, but I managed to get her to stand still while I rinsed her shoulder. It had to hurt, even though it had been an hour or two since the injury occurred. If it had been me, I probably wouldn't want to stand still and get the hose, either.

"Herb, go see if you can find a light bulb," Emma said. "You can't have them trying to sew her up in the dark."

"Oh, no, don't worry about that," I said. I imagined Herb trying to climb a rickety ladder next to the high-strung horse, and shuddered. While some additional light would be a bonus, it wasn't necessary, and we'd probably be done before he got the bulb changed, anyway. "Dr. Lacher's headlamp puts out plenty of light. She'll be fine."

Herb grunted, and I detected an unspoken note of thanks. Emma wasn't so easily deterred. "Are you sure? It's awfully dark out here. I told Herb to change that bulb a year ago, and he hasn't done it yet."

"I'm sure. We might not be able to see much, but she'll be able to see just fine, and that's what counts." Toots snorted, and I returned my attention to her. The barn wasn't really designed for horses. It was more of a storage shed with a walk-through center aisle and open stalls on the side. It had probably been used for sheep or a cow in years past and wasn't used for much of anything now. The low rafters would be dangerous for a horse in distress, so I kept myself between the doorway and Toots as she shifted around.

Erica returned a few minutes later with a tray full of supplies, which she set on the ground just inside the barn door. With the additional light, I could see that the water running down Toots' leg was mostly clear. Erica shut the hose off and came over, pulling a needle out of her pocket.

"I'm going to give her a bit of sedation," she said. "Normally, I wouldn't worry about that, but since she's so reactive, I think it's a good idea."

She uncapped the needle as she stepped across the puddle of bloody water, and Toots lost her mind. She reared up with a squeal, nearly tearing the lead rope out of my hand. My heart tried to leap out of my chest, and I took a quick step back in case she struck out with her front feet. The moment her hooves hit the ground again, Erica went to work on soothing her.

"Whoa, Toots, whoa girl, easy now." She stepped over to me and took the lead rope as Toots backed up nervously. The needle was back in her pocket, and she pulled the clicker out again. Free of my responsibility of holding the rope, I moved back out of the way.

Erica worked her magic, and within a minute or so, Toots dropped her head, which is an indication of relaxation. I heard the clicker click a few more times, and then Erica took the needle out again. Toots raised her head and snorted, but Erica kept up the soothing litany, rubbing the syringe up and down her neck to show her it was okay. I almost missed it when Erica spoke to me.

"I need more treats," she said, not changing her tone. I eased over and gave her a handful out of my pocket.

She continued the process, and I moved back over by Emma and Herb.

"Do you think she'll be able to do it?" Emma asked. "Toots is making it darn near impossible."

"Oh, yeah," I said. "I've seen her do this with a lot of needle-shy horses. Clicker training is amazing."

Emma let out a muffled humph. "I've never seen anyone clicker train a horse. A dog, maybe, but I ain't never seen it done on a horse."

I started to say something, but Herb beat me to it. "She did it out there, got the halter on her with the clicker in two minutes."

Emma didn't say anything, and I smiled in the darkness. People are often resistant to new things, and the best thing we could do here was let her see it for herself. Toots dropped her head as Erica rubbed the capped needle on her neck, and the clicker popped again. Erica put the needle in her mouth and pulled the cap off with her teeth, rubbing Toots' neck with the other hand while keeping a grip on the lead rope. Toots' ear twitched when the needle touched her neck, but she was otherwise still. A second later it was over, and Erica stepped back, patting Toots and giving her praise.

"That's a good girl," she said, capping the needle and sliding it back in her pocket. "We'll give you a minute and let the drugs kick in."

I moved back over and took the lead rope, and Erica pulled on a pair of surgical gloves. She handed me several packs of suture and the needle drivers, which I put in my shirt pocket for easy access. "Okay," she said, pulling another syringe from the tray. "Let's see if we can get the area blocked. She's probably not going to like this much, either."

I shortened my grip on the lead rope as Erica rubbed the syringe on Toots' shoulder beside the wound. Toots stood quietly, and Erica clicked the clicker. She uncapped the needle and began injecting the numbing drug around the edges of the injured area so that Toots wouldn't feel the stitches going in. I was braced for the worst, but with a little bit of sedative on board, Toots didn't seem to care what was going on.

Once everything was numb, Erica slathered petroleum jelly all over the wound and grabbed the clippers. She began trimming the hair away from the edge of the wound, which would allow it to heal faster. The clipped hairs stuck to the jelly, rather than the flesh beneath, and when she was done, she scrubbed the whole area clean with chlorhexidine gauze. A minute later, she was ready to start sewing.

"Needle drivers," she said. I pulled the needle drivers and a suture pack out of my shirt pocket. I gave her the needle drivers, which look like a pair of scissors, except the tips are flat like pliers instead of sharp. When you pick up a needle and squeeze the handles together, they lock in place. It's a whole lot easier to push a needle through the tough, thick skin of a horse that way, rather than with your fingers, especially when you have to do it over and over. Next, I opened the suture pack. Erica grabbed the curved needle with the drivers and locked it on, pulling the needle off the plastic mount. The blue suture string followed, and I tucked the empty pack in my pants pocket.

"Can you grab a glove?" Erica asked. "I'm going to need you to hold this flap in place to get me started." She turned to the side and thrust her hip towards me. I pulled a glove out of her scrub pocket and slipped it on.

"Tell me what to do," I said.

She pulled a set of forceps out of her scrub pocket and adjusted the headlamp. "Lift from the tip and pull it all the way up. Yep, just like that. Hold it there."

I held the lead rope with one hand, and the triangle of skin with the other hand. The rip was pretty impressive. From the top where I was holding it, it went down her shoulder about six inches on the front, and back and down the other way about eight inches. Erica started stitching it in place, and Emma and Herb stepped a bit closer to watch.

It only took about a minute for my hand to start cramping. The skin was slippery, and I had to pinch it pretty hard to keep from losing my grip. I had no way to change hands, so I had to tough it out. Sweat popped out on my forehead, despite the fact that it was after midnight. Erica methodically sewed stitch after stich, working her way up. My arm was numb from the elbow down by the time she told me I could let go, and I wasn't even sure if I was still holding it or not. I shook my hand, trying to force some blood back into it, but I couldn't complain about it. If my hand was sore from holding the flap of skin, I couldn't imagine what hers felt like from holding the needle drivers and forceps.

"I need another suture pack."

I pulled a second pack out of my pocket, but I couldn't grip the flaps to open it up. "Oh, my goodness," I said. "I've got a wimpy hand. I may need your needle drivers to open this thing."

Erica sighed, thrusting the needle drivers into my hand as she grabbed the suture pack and ripped it open. "Remind me to make fun of you later."

"Is it going to be okay?" Emma asked. "It doesn't look so bad, now."

Erica nodded as she began sewing again. "This is going to heal up great. It's going to drain some goo out the bottom for a few days, and we might lose some of this skin, but six months from now, you won't even be able to tell it happened."

"Well, that's a relief," Emma said. "We don't do much with the horses since Karen passed away, but I still hate to see them get hurt."

"Who does your vaccines?" Erica asked. I had a feeling she already knew the answer.

Herb cleared his throat. "Well, I expect they're probably due. We haven't had anyone out since, well, you know, Karen used to handle all that, so…"

I knew exactly what he was trying to say, and I felt bad for him. Trying to deal with the death of your child must be incredibly difficult, and there are a million details to be dealt with. It was no surprise that the horse's healthcare had slipped through the cracks.

"At a minimum, they need to be vaccinated every six months," Erica said. "If you'd like, I can have my office call you tomorrow and get you set up on a schedule. That way, you don't have to remember when they're due."

Emma made the decision immediately. "Yes, that would be wonderful. And you'll have to tell me where I can learn how to use a clicker."

I turned away to hide my smile. Emma had been skeptical about the clicker training, but it seemed that she'd had a change of heart. It happens to most people who see it in action, but it still strikes me as funny how fast people change their mind about it.

I cleaned up our mess and hauled everything to the truck while Erica talked to them about caring for the wound. I could hear the clicker from the truck, and I knew they were getting a crash course in how to use it. I was glad, because they would need to handle Toots every day as she healed. The injury was unfortunate, but if there was a silver lining, it was that Toots would be getting some attention, the horses would start getting vaccines and dental care, and Emma and Herb were learning something new, and that's always a good thing. Working with their daughter's horse might even help them deal with her death. Animals have a way of doing things like that, even the tough ones. Maybe *especially* the tough ones.

The drive home was just as quiet as the drive out. We saw several armadillos and an opossum, but no more deer. On our driveway, we had to wait for a skunk to waddle down the fence line and find a hole to escape through. It's interesting how busy the roads are when the people are at home, asleep. It's a good reminder that we're just one species out of millions living on this planet, and we all have to share the space.

I fell asleep the instant my head hit the pillow. For once, I was able to sleep past 5:00 am, and I woke up to the bellowing of the donkeys at seven. They didn't care that I was up all night. It was breakfast time, and things needed to happen. They were right, of course. That's how it goes.

Chapter 21

FINAL THOUGHTS

THANK YOU FOR READING THIS BOOK! I am incredibly fortunate in so many ways. First and foremost, I have the very best wife in the world. She has given me a life so full of joy and adventure that it makes me feel like I was merely existing in a vacuum before I found her. Not only has she shared her life with me, but by extension, she has also given me the opportunity to share in moments of other people's lives with their animals. Hopefully, by now, you know what a big deal that is.

As I said at the end of my first book of horse adventures, horse people are different. The commonality of that special relationship that horse people share with their horses can transcend religion, politics, and every other social division that people use to separate themselves. I'm sure that there are rivalries between various disciplines, as horse people are still human beings, but those things don't stop horse people from feeling a little ping in their heart when they pass a horse trailer going down the road, or hear of a tragedy involving a horse. I've done a lot of things in my life, and lived a lot of places, and I've never found another group of people like horse people.

Since the release of *Adventures of the Horse Doctor's Husband* in September 2019, I've talked to a lot of people about the books, and about horse life. Many of the people I've met are older, and no longer have horses. They tell me about the way these stories took them back and helped them remember times with their horses that they'd forgotten about. Sharing in these moments with people is magic, and it is one of the most fulfilling things I've ever experienced.

I get emails and Facebook messages from people telling me how much they enjoyed reading about my relationship with Erica, too, and that always makes me smile. I didn't intend for these books to be a love story. I just wanted to make sure you realize how amazing Erica is, and that you know I'm not taking her for granted. Her mission is to make the world a better place for horses, and I am in awe of her commitment to that. She expresses it in so many ways, whether it's talking to clients about their horses, hosting free seminars at our veterinary clinic, recording podcasts to educate people all over the world about equine healthcare, or just the way she treats her own horses. She commits so much of her time to learning more about horses, both on the medical front and on the training front, and she loves sharing what she learns with others. She's a wonderful human being, and I am just tickled pink that she picked me to share her life with.

One last thing about these books. A lot of people have noted that I don't talk about the abuse and neglect that runs rampant in the horse world. That is not by accidental omission. I am very much aware of that stuff, as I think most people are, at least, people who have been inside the horse world for a long time. I chose not to talk about it, not to diminish the importance of combatting it, but rather, because I want to put something positive and fulfilling into the world. Social media is filled with groups of people committed to exposing atrocities and rescuing horses from bad situations, and I think those are good places to talk about that stuff. With my books, I just want to share the things that remind us that there is good in the world. Sometimes it's painful, like when we lose an animal, but it hurts precisely because the relationship with them was so wonderful. It's that relationship that I'm trying to highlight. Even the crazy goat lady loved her goats the same as I love Gerald. The situation was wildly entertaining, at least to me, but the common denominator was there, and that's the commitment to providing for the animal. I hope that came through to you, as the reader.

So, that's it for this go around. I hope you enjoyed tagging along with me on these adventures. If you're able, I'd love to get a review from you wherever you bought the book! It helps other people decide if it's a book they'd enjoy. I would also like to invite you to find our veterinary clinic on Facebook and follow us there. We post all kinds of great material, whether it's entertaining, educational, or both. You can find us at **Facebook.com/SpringhillEquine.**

Thank you again for sharing your time with me!
Justin B. Long

About The Author

JUSTIN B. LONG is a self-embracing nerd who loves crunching numbers, researching interesting things, and listening to podcasts, in addition to reading loads of books. By day he is the CFO of Springhill Equine Veterinary Clinic, and by night he is a science fiction author. When he's not responding to after-hours horse emergencies or dreaming up alternate dimensions of reality, he enjoys hiking in national parks. He lives near Gainesville, Florida on a small farm with his incredible wife, 7 horses, 5 cats, 2 donkeys, 2 dogs, and a sheep named Gerald.